HANSEN LECTURESHIP SERIES

CHRISTINE A. COLÓN

CHOOSING COMMUNITY

ACTION, FAITH, AND
JOY IN THE WORKS OF
Dorothy L. Sayers

An imprint of InterVarsity Press
Downers Grove, Illinois

InterVarsity Press
P.O. Box 1400, Downers Grove, IL 60515-1426
ivpress.com
email@ivpress.com

©2019 by The Marion E. Wade Center

All rights reserved. No part of this book may be reproduced in any form without written permission from InterVarsity Press.

InterVarsity Press® is the book-publishing division of InterVarsity Christian Fellowship/USA®, a movement of students and faculty active on campus at hundreds of universities, colleges, and schools of nursing in the United States of America, and a member movement of the International Fellowship of Evangelical Students. For information about local and regional activities, visit intervarsity.org.

Scripture quotations, unless otherwise noted, are from The Holy Bible, English Standard Version, copyright © 2001 by Crossway Bibles, a division of Good News Publishers. Used by permission. All rights reserved.

All interior photographs used by permission of the Marion E. Wade Center, Wheaton College, Wheaton, IL.

Interior images of letters by Dorothy L. Sayers used by permission of the estate of Dorothy L. Sayers, represented by David Higham Associates, Ltd.

Cover design: David Fassett
Interior design: Daniel van Loon
Cover images: Dorothy Leigh Sayers: © Pictorial Press Ltd. / Alamy Stock Photo
    Recycled background: © Zakharova_Natalia

ISBN 978-0-8308-5374-8 (print)
ISBN 978-0-8308-7030-1 (digital)

InterVarsity Press is committed to ecological stewardship and to the conservation of natural resources in all our operations. This book was printed using sustainably sourced paper.

Library of Congress Cataloging-in-Publication Data
Names: Colón, Christine A., 1968- author.
Title: Choosing community : action, faith, and joy in the works of Dorothy L. Sayers / Christine A. Colón.
Description: Downers Grove : IVP Academic 2019. | Series: Hansen lectureship series | Includes bibliographical references and index.
Identifiers: LCCN 2019027280 (print) | LCCN 2019027281 (ebook) | ISBN 9780830853748 (paperback) | ISBN 9780830870301 (ebook)
Subjects: LCSH: Sayers, Dorothy L. (Dorothy Leigh), 1893-1957--Criticism and interpretation. | Communities in literature.
Classification: LCC PR6037.A95 Z626 2019 (print) | LCC PR6037.A95 (ebook) | DDC 823/.912—dc23
LC record available at https://lccn.loc.gov/2019027280
LC ebook record available at https://lccn.loc.gov/2019027281

| P | 22 | 21 | 20 | 19 | 18 | 17 | 16 | 15 | 14 | 13 | 12 | 11 | 10 | 9 | 8 | 7 | 6 | 5 | 4 | 3 | 2 | 1 |
| Y | 39 | 38 | 37 | 36 | 35 | 34 | 33 | 32 | 31 | 30 | 29 | 28 | 27 | 26 | 25 | 24 | 23 | 22 | 21 | 20 | 19 |

"Christine Colón has written an original and thoroughly fascinating book on Dorothy L. Sayers and community. Sayers enthusiasts will appreciate her meticulous research, but even the general reader who doesn't know Sayers will learn something about how people can live together in harmony despite the traumas of this world."

Suzanne Bray, professor of English, Lille Catholic University

"This is a fascinating study by Christine Colón using examples from Dorothy L. Sayers's fiction, drama, and theological writings to demonstrate her belief in action, faith, and joy in community. I commend it."

Alan F. Jesson, Dorothy L. Sayers Society Committee

"This book is itself a satisfying act of community: Colón and her commentators draw out and riff on the Sayersian themes of communal action, faith, and joy in a way that the reader can sense—and join—the original dynamic of live lecture and response. Colón makes illuminating connections between various works of Sayers, showing a firm grasp of the canon of Sayers's detective and dramatic writing, and makes a compelling case for the breadth and rightness to Sayers's thinking about community. Kriner, Mangin, and McGraw draw out the life and implications of this vision of community for their own disciplines of literary analysis, drama, and politics—the kind of discussions that Sayers herself would have relished. This book is a pleasing and meaty communal conversation with Sayers."

Kathryn Wehr, Sayers scholar, Anselm House, St. Paul, Minnesota

"Christine Colón has provided an engaging argument for the importance of community in the astonishingly varied literary corpus of Dorothy L. Sayers. Colón's insightful tracking of this theme through Sayers's detective fiction, religious drama, theatrical associations, and epistolary friendships illuminates both the mind of this significant author and the importance of the community life that Sayers's life so remarkably exemplified. The book is an especially winsome account of an important author and a crucial theme in lives well lived."

Mark Noll, Francis A. McAnaney Professor of History, emeritus, University of Notre Dame

"In this insightful and engaging book, Christine Colón reveals the importance of a Christian conception of community to the life and work of Dorothy L. Sayers: it is built into the very stonework of Sayers's plays and reverberates through the landscapes of her detective stories. Reading Colón's reflections on Sayers, we are reminded that this understanding of community is a rich and dynamic one, indeed—bound up with questions of vocation, the truth of doctrine, and the delights of friendship and camaraderie. Whether you are looking for a guide to Sayers's work or a thoughtful meditation on Christian life together, you will not be disappointed. Colón's scholarship sheds light on Sayers's writings while inviting us to reflect more deeply on our relationships with one another."

James E. Beitler III, associate professor of English, Wheaton College, author of *Seasoned Speech: Rhetoric in the Life of the Church*

"Colón wends her way through Sayers's detective novels and religious plays in the context of her life and times to help us see what Sayers wanted us to learn about community and the work that God has given each of us to do with joy for the health of our communities—especially the church. Sayers comes through as one who passionately grounded these insights in essential Christian doctrines, such as God's triune existence and the atonement, during times of war and societal decay. At a time when we seem to be sinking into tribalism in a contentious world, there are lessons to be gleaned from Sayers thanks to Colón's guidance. And this study might just prompt one to hurry to the bookshelf and read or reread a Sayers piece, seeing in it what otherwise would have been missed."

Dennis Okholm, professor of theology, Azusa Pacific University, author of *Learning Theology Through the Church's Worship*

"Christine A. Colón's new book about Dorothy L. Sayers enriches one's experience and appreciation of even very dear and familiar texts, provoking numerous, Why, of course! moments of illumination and affirming one's sense of home in the Sayers universe. A happy and stimulating combination of the scholarly and eminently readable, this book weaves in and out of Sayers's fiction and personal experience, not only convincingly demonstrating the important dimension of community in her novels and plays but also challenging one to think of the quality and the role of community in one's own life and work. It powerfully reminds us yet again of Sayers's lucid intellect, bold expression, and brilliant humor. Strong and thoughtful responses from a wider community of thinkers, each throwing professional light on various aspects of Dr. Colón's lectures, only strengthen the central thrust of the book and prove yet again the vital role of community in any truly human creative endeavor."

Olga B. Lukmanova, associate professor of English, N. A. Dobrolubov Linguistics University, Nizhny Novgorod, Russia

"Professor Colón has given us a new way to appreciate Sayers's depth as a writer and opened ways for us to think about community that are sorely needed today. This is a great introduction to Sayers's writing and also an excellent book for readers who know and love Sayers as a detective novelist or as a religious writer. It brings these dimensions of Sayers's work together and shows the breadth and depth of Sayers's insight into Christianity and community."

Christine Fletcher, associate professor of theology, Benedictine University

"*Choosing Community* brings together four different voices in a dynamic polyphony. The interactive structure of the text constitutes a diversity in unity reflective of the social harmony admired by Dorothy Sayers. What results is a fresh approach to this brilliant woman writer who wrote on the margins of the Inklings and regaled C. S. Lewis with Austen-inspired tales of her poultry. The book is full of interesting facts from Sayers's historical context and is a delight from beginning to end. The writers model an intelligent civility much needed in today's cultural discourse."

Natasha Duquette, author of *Veiled Intent*, professor and chair, English department, Tyndale University College

To all the students I have taught
in my courses on Dorothy L. Sayers.

Thank you for going on this
journey of discovery with me.

CONTENTS

ACKNOWLEDGMENTS .... *ix*

INTRODUCTION
Walter Hansen .... *xi*

ABBREVIATIONS .... *xix*

1 Dorothy L. Sayers's Vision
   for Communities of Action 1
   Response: Tiffany Eberle Kriner

2 Dorothy L. Sayers's Vision
   for Communities of Faith 41
   Response: Andy Mangin

3 Dorothy L. Sayers's Vision
   for Communities of Joy 82
   Response: Bryan T. McGraw

CONTRIBUTORS *128*

AUTHOR INDEX *129*

SUBJECT INDEX *130*

Acknowledgments

I **WOULD LIKE TO EXPRESS MY GRATITUDE** to all those who participated in helping this book become a reality: Walter and Darlene Hansen for their support of the Wade Center and the Hansen lectures, Marjorie Lamp Mead for her advice as I was planning the lectures, Laura Schmidt and Carolyn Greco for their help with the research and the images, David Higham Associates for granting me permission to quote extracts and reproduce sketches from Dorothy L. Sayers's unpublished letters, my three respondents—Tiffany Kriner, Andy Mangin, and Bryan McGraw—for their insightful reflections, David McNutt for seeing the book through production, and finally, the late Chris Mitchell for encouraging me to explore the Sayers Papers in the first place.

INTRODUCTION TO THE HANSEN LECTURESHIP SERIES

Walter Hansen

COMMUNAL FLOURISHING

By all accounts, Dorothy L. Sayers, the English novelist, playwright, and poet, was a gifted writer and a somewhat eccentric figure, not unlike some of her own characters. Barbara Reynolds, her primary biographer, records this evaluation of Sayers:

> What a woman! Brilliant, erratic, rude and impatient as only dedicated writers and artists can be, earnest, hard-working, loving, yet never achieving settled love, deeply religious, with a flair for expressing old truths in new words, funny as well as witty, eccentric, curious in appearance, scholarly, a woman who knew her own mind and knew, too, that it was as good as any man's; a fighter who could be a worthy opponent in any kind of controversy.[1]

In light of her own articulations of Christianity, perhaps "defender of the faith" is another title that could be applied to Sayers.

---

[1] Rosamund Essex, quoted in Barbara Reynolds, *Dorothy L. Sayers: Her Life and Soul* (New York: St. Martin's, 1993), 367.

A central element of the Christian faith is the importance of community, as diverse people are brought together through the Holy Spirit to be the one body of Christ.

In the first of her three lectures on the communal vision of Dorothy Sayers, Christine Colón discusses Sayers's growth as a writer as demonstrated in her Lord Peter Wimsey novels, specifically through her portrayal of the roles of individuals who threaten or restore the health of the community. I have enjoyed reading these detective novels, but I had never considered that it is possible to trace Sayers's growth in her work as a writer by investigating the trajectory of her novels.

The importance of community was also a theme in Sayers's own life. She benefited from the communities of fellow writers, such as those in the Detection Club, a group of detective fiction authors that included G. K. Chesterton, among others. In Chesterton's estimation, "[Sayers] sustains about the best level, in my opinion, of lively and intelligent writing in this style."[2] Notably, Sayers was not an official member of the Inklings, the famous writing group that included C. S. Lewis, J. R. R. Tolkien, Charles Williams, and others, but she was friends with Lewis and Williams. Moreover, she carried on extensive correspondence with many people, and she lauded the theater, a community that she discovered with the stage production of *Busman's Honeymoon* in 1936 and later at the Canterbury Festival.

However, one community in which Sayers evidently did not find much support for her work was the church. Here is how she described the church's approach to artists:

> The church's approach to an intelligent carpenter is usually confined to exhorting him to not be drunk and disorderly in his leisure hours, and to come to church on Sundays. What the church

---

[2]Chesterton, "The Detection Club," *The Strand Magazine*, #509 (May 1933), 468.

should be telling him is this: that the very first demand that his religion makes upon him is that he should make good tables.³

Before we dismiss these claims as uninformed, we should recall that Sayers's father, the Reverend Henry Sayers, was Rector of Bluntisham and later Christchurch in the Fenlands, so she speaks as a "daughter of the Manse" who knew the realities of church life, perhaps all too well. Sayers considered her work as a writer to be a sacred task, but she did not hear the church value the work of artists. She bitterly laments that "the church will tolerate, or permit, a pious intention to excuse work so ugly, so pretentious, so tawdry and twaddling, so insincere and insipid, so *bad* as to shock and horrify any decent draftsman."⁴ According to Sayers, the reason the church does not encourage artists to pursue excellence in their work is that "she has forgotten that the secular vocation is sacred. Forgotten that a building must be good architecture before it can be a good church; that a painting must be well painted before it can be a good sacred picture; that work must be good work before it can call itself God's work."⁵

Sayers's devastating critique of the church's negative attitude toward works of art and the work of artists is a theme in her essays. Fortunately, that is not the theme of Professor Colón's lectures. Instead, she emphasizes the positive directions found in Sayers's work for building true communities where individuals joyfully support each other in their God-given work, a vision that applies to the church as well as other communities. All who seek the welfare of their communities will find reliable guidance by following Colón's exploration of the dramatic,

---

³Dorothy L. Sayers, "Why Work?" in *Creed or Chaos?* (London: Methuen & Co. Ltd., 1947), 58.
⁴Sayers, "Why Work?," 59.
⁵Sayers, "Why Work?," 59.

eccentric, and whimsical vision of Dorothy Sayers for Christians living and working together in healthy community.

The Ken and Jean Hansen Lectureship

I was motivated to set up a lectureship in honor of my parents, Ken and Jean Hansen, at the Wade Center primarily because they loved Marion E. Wade. My father began working for Mr. Wade in 1946, the year I was born. He launched my father's career and mentored him in business. Often when I look at the picture of Marion Wade in the Wade Center, I give thanks to God for his beneficial influence in my family and in my life.

After Darlene and I were married in December 1967, the middle of my senior year at Wheaton College, we invited Marion and Lil Wade for dinner in our apartment. I wanted Darlene to get to know the best storyteller I've ever heard.

When Marion Wade passed through death into the Lord's presence on November 28, 1973, his last words to my father were, "Remember Joshua, Ken." As Joshua was the one who followed Moses to lead God's people, my father was the one who followed Marion Wade to lead the ServiceMaster Company.

After members of Marion Wade's family and friends at ServiceMaster set up a memorial fund in honor of Marion Wade at Wheaton College, my parents initiated the renaming of Clyde Kilby's collection of papers and books from the seven British authors—C. S. Lewis, J. R. R. Tolkien, Dorothy L. Sayers, George MacDonald, G. K. Chesterton, Charles Williams, and Owen Barfield—as the Marion E. Wade Collection.

I'm also motivated to name this lectureship after my parents because they loved the literature of these seven authors whose papers are now collected at the Wade Center.

Introduction to the Hansen Lectureship Series

While I was still in college, my father and mother took an evening course on Lewis and Tolkien with Dr. Kilby. The class was limited to nine students so that they could meet in Dr. Kilby's living room. Dr. Kilby's wife, Martha, served tea and cookies.

My parents were avid readers, collectors, and promoters of the books of the seven Wade authors, even hosting a book club in their living room led by Dr. Kilby. When they moved to Santa Barbara in 1977, they named their home Rivendell, after the beautiful house of the elf Lord Elrond, whose home served as a welcome haven to weary travelers as well as a cultural center for Middle-earth history and lore. Family and friends who stayed in their home know that their home fulfilled Tolkien's description of Rivendell:

> And so at last they all came to the Last Homely House, and found its doors flung wide. . . . [The] house was perfect whether you liked food, or sleep, or work, or story-telling, or singing, or just sitting and thinking best, or a pleasant mixture of them all. . . . Their clothes were mended as well as their bruises, their tempers and their hopes. . . . Their plans were improved with the best advice.[6]

Our family treasures many memories of our times at Rivendell, highlighted by storytelling. Our conversations often drew from images of the stories of Lewis, Tolkien, and the other authors. We had our own code language: "That was a terrible Bridge of Khazad-dûm experience." "That meeting felt like the Council of Elrond."

One cold February, Clyde and Martha Kilby escaped the deep freeze of Wheaton to thaw out and recover for two weeks at my parents' Rivendell home in Santa Barbara. As a thank-you note, Clyde Kilby dedicated his book *Images of Salvation in the Fiction of C. S. Lewis* to

---

[6]J. R. R. Tolkien, *The Hobbit* (London: Unwin Hyman, 1987), 50-51.

my parents. When my parents set up our family foundation in 1985, they named the foundation Rivendell Stewards' Trust.

In many ways, they lived in and lived out the stories of the seven authors. It seems fitting and proper, therefore, to name this lectureship in honor of Ken and Jean Hansen.

Escape for Prisoners

The purpose of the Hansen Lectureship is to provide a way of escape for prisoners. J. R. R. Tolkien writes about the positive role of escape in literature:

> I have claimed that Escape is one of the main functions of fairy-stories, and since I do not disapprove of them, it is plain that I do not accept the tone of scorn or pity with which "Escape" is now so often used: a tone for which the uses of the word outside literary criticism give no warrant at all. In what the misusers of Escape are fond of calling Real Life, Escape is evidently as a rule very practical, and may even be heroic.[7]

Note that Tolkien is not talking about escap*ism* or an avoidance of reality but rather the idea of escape as a means of providing a new view of reality, the true, transcendent reality that is often screened from our view in this fallen world. He adds:

> Evidently we are faced by a misuse of words, and also by a confusion of thought. Why should a man be scorned, if, finding himself in prison, he tries to get out and go home? Or if, when he cannot do so, he thinks and talks about other topics than jailers and prison-walls? The world outside has not

---

[7] J. R. R. Tolkien, "On Fairy-Stories," in *Tales from the Perilous Realm* (Boston: Houghton Mifflin, 2008), 375.

become less real because the prisoner cannot see it. In using Escape in this [derogatory] way the [literary] critics have chosen the wrong word, and, what is more, they are confusing, not always by sincere error, the Escape of the Prisoner with the Flight of the Deserter.[8]

I am not proposing that these lectures give us a way to escape from our responsibilities or ignore the needs of the world around us but rather that we explore the stories of the seven authors to escape from a distorted view of reality, from a sense of hopelessness, and to awaken us to the true hope of what God desires for us and promises to do for us.

C. S. Lewis offers a similar vision for the possibility that such literature could open our eyes to a new reality:

> We want to escape the illusions of perspective.... We want to see with other eyes, to imagine with other imaginations, to feel with other hearts, as well as with our own....
>
> The man who is contented to be only himself, and therefore less a self, is in prison. My own eyes are not enough for me, I will see through those of others....
>
> In reading great literature I become a thousand men yet remain myself.... Here as in worship, in love, in moral action, and in knowing, I transcend myself; and am never more myself than when I do.[9]

The purpose of the Hansen Lectureship is to explore the great literature of the seven Wade authors so that we can escape from the prison of our self-centeredness and narrow, parochial perspective in order to

---

[8]Tolkien, "On Fairy-Stories," 376.
[9]C. S. Lewis, *An Experiment in Criticism* (Cambridge: Cambridge University, 1965), 137, 140-41.

see with other eyes, feel with other hearts, and be equipped for practical deeds in real life.

As a result, we will learn new ways to experience and extend the fulfillment of our Lord's mission: "to proclaim freedom for the prisoners and recovery of sight for the blind, to set the oppressed free" (Lk 4:18 NIV).

ABBREVIATIONS

BH	Dorothy L. Sayers, *Busman's Honeymoon* (New York: Harper, 1995).
EC	Dorothy L. Sayers, *The Emperor Constantine* (Grand Rapids: Eerdmans, 1976).
GN	Dorothy L. Sayers, *Gaudy Night* (New York: Harper, 1995).
HHC	Dorothy L. Sayers, *Have His Carcase* (New York: Harper, 1995).
JV	Dorothy L. Sayers, *The Just Vengeance* (London: Gollancz, 1946).
MMA	Dorothy L. Sayers, *Murder Must Advertise* (New York: Harper, 1995).
NT	Dorothy L. Sayers, *The Nine Tailors* (New York: Harvest/Harcourt, 1962).
SP	Dorothy L. Sayers, *Strong Poison* (New York: Harper, 1995).
UBC	Dorothy L. Sayers, *The Unpleasantness at the Bellona Club* (New York: Harper, 1995).
WB	Dorothy L. Sayers, *Whose Body?* (New York: Harper, 1995).
ZH	Dorothy L. Sayers, *The Zeal of Thy House* (Eugene, OR: Wipf & Stock, 2011).

DOROTHY L. SAYERS'S VISION FOR COMMUNITIES OF ACTION

*I*N THE NINE TAILORS, one of her most famous detective novels, Dorothy L. Sayers discusses the "art of change-ringing"—an art where a group of bell ringers gather together in a church's bell tower "to work out mathematical permutations and combinations" on the bells.[1] Rather than playing tunes on the bells, change ringers carefully practice various peals—sequences of different combinations of the order of the bells. For each unique peal of the bells, a change ringer must understand where his or her particular bell falls within the ever-shifting pattern and then must be able to control the bell well enough to make sure that it rings at the correct moment. Take, for example, the peal known as Plain Bob Minor, which is played on six bells numbered from the highest pitch to the lowest. The peal begins with each bell ringing in order, but as it progresses, the order of the bells shifts:

1 2 3 4 5 6
2 1 4 3 6 5
2 4 1 6 3 5

---

[1] Dorothy L. Sayers, *The Nine Tailors* (New York: Harvest/Harcourt, 1962), 22.

4 2 6 1 5 3
4 6 2 5 1 3
6 4 5 2 3 1, etc.[2]

To an untrained ear, these changes in the order can be difficult to perceive, but for a change ringer each peal makes its own particular music. As you might suspect, this art is not an easy one to master. It requires not only the physical stamina to pull a heavy church bell, sometimes for hours at a time, but also the mental stamina to keep track of when to pull your bell in the ever-shifting patterns that make up a peal. It also requires that you work in perfect harmony with everyone else in the group, timing your bell ringing in relation to everyone else's. There are, in fact, so many different components involved in change ringing that it has the potential to quickly deteriorate into chaos. When everything comes together, however, there is, as Sayers's narrator describes it in *The Nine Tailors*, "satisfaction in mathematical completeness and mechanical perfection . . . [and] the solemn intoxication that comes of intricate ritual faultlessly performed."[3]

I begin with the example of change ringing because I believe it serves as a powerful image of the challenges of community that Sayers explores throughout her works. Like change ringing, community for Sayers is an "intricate ritual" in which individuals must work diligently to perform their parts, trusting that these parts will ultimately combine well with the others so that the ritual will be "faultlessly performed." In these essays, I will be exploring how Sayers articulates three particular qualities that she believes are essential in order to successfully perform this ritual of community: action, faith, and joy. Because Sayers returns

---

[2]YouTube has a number of examples of change ringing. To hear "Plain Bob Minor," watch "Tamworth—Plain Bob Minor" at www.youtu.be/85Fr8p7feS8.
[3]*NT*, 22-23.

to the topic of community so many times throughout her works, I believe it can serve as a powerful lens through which we may gain not only a good sense of Sayers's artistry but also a deeper understanding of some of the theological foundations of her work.

In her introduction to *The Man Born to Be King*, her retelling of the life of Christ, Sayers discusses how closely theology and artistry are intertwined. She remarks, "A loose and sentimental theology begets loose and sentimental artforms; an illogical theology lands one in illogical situations; an ill-balanced theology issues in false emphasis and absurdity."[4] While Sayers is focused here primarily on the process of adapting Scripture to literature, she had earlier made a similar connection between theological truth and the creative mind in *The Mind of the Maker*.[5] For Sayers, her integrity as an artist was enmeshed with her integrity as a Christian, and this was true not simply of her religious plays and essays but also of her detective novels. I will begin this series of essays, then, by focusing on how Sayers's growth as a writer of detective fiction is integrally connected to her developing ideas regarding community and, more particularly, the role of individual action within it. As

Figure 1. Sayers as a successful writer

---

[4]Dorothy L. Sayers, *The Man Born to Be King* (San Francisco: Ignatius, 1990), 13.
[5]Dorothy L. Sayers, *The Mind of the Maker* (New York: Harper, 1979).

Sayers worked to develop the genre beyond the simple puzzle that often characterized it, she also began developing a more complex theological perspective on community—one that would resonate powerfully throughout her life and work.

Community in Sayers's Life

In her own life, Sayers was well aware of the potential power of strong community. At university, she and several of her friends created the Mutual Admiration Society, a writing group where members would come together to share their poetry and invite critique from the other members. As a detective novelist, she was one of the founding members of the Detection Club, where mystery writers would socialize and support each other in their craft. As a playwright, she

Figure 2. Sayers (second from the right) with friends at college

reveled in the community that arose around each production, immersing herself in the vibrant creativity of the actors, director, and production team. And as a Christian apologist, she worked with St. Anne's House in Soho to open a dialogue between Christians and agnostics through lectures, debates, and discussions. Throughout her life, Sayers immersed herself in groups that would not only help to nurture her own individual creativity but also allow her to work with others to achieve more as a group than she could individually. She recognized the potential power of people working well in community and utilized it in her own life and career.

Sayers was also intensely aware of the problems that arose when people could not figure out how to live well in community, a fact that was vividly revealed to the world through the realities of World War I and World War II. Born in 1893, Sayers was twenty-one years old when World War I erupted. She was, in fact, on a cycling tour of France, and her letters home reveal her excitement about being in the midst of things (as well as her obliviousness to the potential danger). In a letter on August 2, 1914, she remarks,

> Yesterday we went into the town here. It was most extraordinary. Everybody one met seemed to be in a fearful hurry, and on the other hand, all the street corners were occupied by groups of people talking about the war. Every other man had a newspaper in his hands. Soldiers and sailors were all over the place. . . . In the circumstances, you see it is quite possible we may have to come back, if we can get back. I do hope we shall be able to stay, because it is so fearfully thrilling, but of course it wouldn't be fair to stay and eat up all Mme Larnaudie's provisions.[6]

---

[6]Dorothy L. Sayers, *The Letters of Dorothy L. Sayers 1899 to 1936: The Making of a Detective Novelist*, ed. Barbara Reynolds (New York: St. Martin's, 1995), 92.

That excitement began to dim when she returned to England and experienced some of the realities of war, enduring zeppelin raids while a teacher in the port city of Hull and seeing young men return from the front with physical, mental, and emotional wounds. When World War II broke out twenty years later, she began to reflect on the ways that these two wars might be a result of moving away from God's original design for community.

She expressed these ideas in a work written at the outset of the war titled *Begin Here*, in which she argues that the essential challenge of Western society "has been that of inventing and maintaining a kind of state in which every man and woman should enjoy freedom and equality while yet sharing in an orderly communal life."[7] In this work, which was designed to encourage her readers to persevere in the face of war, Sayers approaches the topic from a theological perspective. She first argues that humanity has continually failed to develop community according to God's fundamental laws for the universe and then posits a better approach to community that would bring society closer into alignment with God's original plan. Sayers's approach is founded on the idea that if individuals could learn

Figure 3. Sayers during World War II

---

[7]Dorothy L. Sayers, *Begin Here: A War-Time Essay* (London: Victor Gollancz, 1941), 33.

to integrate "feeling, thought, and deed; soul, mind and body," they would restore the "full creative power" that God designed them to have.[8] Then, they would be able to come together and use that creative power to discover and implement effective solutions for their larger communities. At the time Sayers wrote *Begin Here*, she was known primarily as a writer of detective fiction, so her readers may have been surprised that she not only addressed such a serious and important subject but also discussed it in theological terms. The truth is, Sayers had already been exploring many of these ideas in her fiction writing. She may not have expressed them in explicitly theological terms, but, looking back from the perspective of her later works in Christian apologetics, we can see that many of her ideas about the relationship between individuals and their community develop over the course of her detective novels.

CONVENTIONS OF DETECTIVE FICTION

In order to understand how Sayers was handling the topic of community in her novels, we must first understand the conventions of detective fiction that she was working with. In the standard formula for detective fiction, the story begins with a peaceful, happy family or community that is threatened in some way by evil. The community calls upon a brilliant detective—often accompanied by a less brilliant sidekick—who discovers the evil and purges it from the community so that the community may return to its quiet, peaceful state. While there are certainly variations to this standard formula, it proved to be very popular from the nineteenth century—when the detective novel was created—through the golden age of detective fiction in the 1920s and '30s when Sayers was writing.

---

[8]Sayers, *Begin Here*, 151.

Think, for instance, of a typical Sherlock Holmes mystery such as "The Adventure of the Speckled Band."[9] Here, a young woman in distress arrives to ask Holmes for help. She fears that her stepfather may have killed her sister two years previously and worries that he is now attempting to kill her. Holmes, along with Watson (who recounts the tale), travels to the country estate and carefully examines the evidence. Becoming suspicious of the layout of this young woman's bedroom, Holmes arranges for her to spend the night elsewhere while he, unbeknownst to the stepfather, occupies the chamber and discovers the intricate device that the stepfather had created to encourage a deadly snake—the speckled band of the title—to enter the room and bite whoever happened to be lying in the bed. Holmes, of course, escapes being bitten, and the snake, returning to its handler (the stepfather), bites him instead. At the end of the story, not only has the mystery of the earlier murder been solved, but the evil stepfather who was willing to murder his stepdaughters to control his late wife's fortune has also been destroyed, leaving the young woman free to enjoy the money she has inherited and to marry the man she loves.

As numerous critics of the detective story have pointed out, this formula is problematic, for it presents a simplistic view both of evil and of community. W. H. Auden's critique is one of the most famous. In an article titled "The Guilty Vicarage," Auden begins by outlining two typical trajectories of a detective story and explaining the various components that make up both formulas. The first begins with a "peaceful state before murder" and then moves through the stages of "murder," "false clues, secondary murder, etc.," "solution," and "arrest

---

[9] Arthur Conan Doyle, "The Adventure of the Speckled Band," in *The Complete Original Illustrated Sherlock Holmes* (Secaucus, NJ: Castle, 1976), 108-23.

of murderer" before reaching the "peaceful state after arrest."[10] The second begins with "false innocence" and then moves through the stages of "revelation of presence of guilt," "false location of guilt," "location of real guilt," and "catharsis," ending with a final state of "true innocence."[11] As you can see, the mysteries in both trajectories move through a state of confusion in order to reach a final state of peaceful innocence. The evil has been purged, and the community returns to normal. The question that arises, though, is whether this final state is actually normal, or if it presents a problematic view of the world. As Auden continues, he analyzes his own addiction to detective fiction and presents his suspicion that "the typical reader of detective stories is . . . a person who suffers from a sense of sin"[12] and who enjoys "the illusion of being dissociated from the murderer."[13] For him, detective fiction is a "phantasy of being restored to the Garden of Eden, to a state of innocence."[14] Rather than having to grapple with the evil inside themselves, readers are able to project it entirely upon the fictional villain who is safely eliminated at the end of the story. Sayers herself recognizes this problem, for in *The Mind of the Maker*, she warns her readers that the challenges of real life are not as easily solved as the problems in a detective novel. In fact, she presents a rather harsh condemnation of the genre, declaring, "The detective problem summons us to the energetic exercise of our wits precisely in order that, when we have read the last page, we may sit back in our chairs and cease thinking."[15] Sayers, like Auden, worries that the

---

[10] W. H. Auden, "The Guilty Vicarage: Notes on the Detective Story, by an Addict," *Harper's Magazine*, May 1948, 407.
[11] Auden, "The Guilty Vicarage," 407.
[12] Auden, "The Guilty Vicarage," 411.
[13] Auden, "The Guilty Vicarage," 412.
[14] Auden, "The Guilty Vicarage," 412.
[15] Sayers, *Mind of the Maker*, 205.

escapism of detective fiction encourages readers to avoid the hard challenges of dealing with the realities of evil in themselves and in the world around them.

Sayers's condemnation seems rather harsh, particularly for someone who made her living for many years as a writer of detective fiction, so it is important to realize that from the beginning Sayers recognized the potential for detective fiction to be more than escapism. In her essay "Gaudy Night," Sayers describes the process she went through as she tried to move from the simple formula of a typical detective puzzle to a detective novel of manners: a novel that retained the intrigue of the puzzle but also portrayed a realistic society with complex characters and themes that would compel readers to reflect on the issues of the novel long after they closed the book. This process is a complex one that revolves around the specific ways she crafts her characters and interacts with the conventions of the detective novel.[16] But what I find particularly interesting is how deeply it is intertwined with this issue of community. By investigating the trajectory of her novels, we can begin to see how Sayers asks her readers to rethink the simplistic portrayals of the community and the detective that are part of the traditional formula for mystery novels, encouraging them to reflect on the role that each individual might play in the process of maintaining a healthy community.

Rethinking Community in the Detective Novel

Sayer's early novels are fairly traditional, following the standard formula in which one evil individual threatens the community until

---

[16]For a detailed discussion of how Sayers utilizes and revises nineteenth-century conventions of detective fiction, see chapters 3–5 in my book *Writing for the Masses: Dorothy L. Sayers and the Victorian Literary Tradition* (New York: Routledge, 2018).

he or she is purged from society through the interventions of a brilliant detective, namely, Lord Peter Wimsey. In *Whose Body?* (1923), Sayers's first novel, Peter uncovers the complex maneuverings of a villain who attempts to prove his theories about the criminal mind by orchestrating the perfect murder.[17] Once he is caught, everything returns to normal. Although the family grieves over the death of the victim, they move on with their lives. In fact, the victim's daughter eventually marries one of Peter's friends. The evil has been purged, and the community is restored to its original state of innocence. In her second novel, *Clouds of Witness* (1926), the story is a little more complex, for the presumed murder of Denis Cathcart reveals the infidelity and lies that already exist within the community.[18] Here, the original community is not entirely innocent, but, interestingly, the overall structure of the novel remains the same. By discovering the truth about Cathcart's death, Peter not only saves his brother from being convicted of murder but also purges the community of their infidelity and lies by bringing these issues to light and provoking the real villain in this community to the actions that lead to his death. With her first two novels, then, Sayers closely follows the conventions that Auden would later outline in his diagrams, for the role of the detective is simply to return these two communities to their state of innocence.

In a number of her later novels, however, Sayers begins to challenge these simplistic views of community and evil. In these novels, the communities are not essentially peaceful and good, nor are the problems easily resolved simply by finding the true villain. Here, evil—whether social or moral—pervades the community, making it much

---

[17]Dorothy L. Sayers, *Whose Body?* (New York: Harper, 1995).
[18]Dorothy L. Sayers, *Clouds of Witness* (New York: Harper, 1995).

more difficult for the brilliant detective to bring the community to a state of innocence. For example, in *The Unpleasantness at the Bellona Club* (1928), Sayers initially seems to follow the traditional formula: a greedy villain throws the community into chaos by murdering an elderly man in order to gain access to a substantial inheritance, and Peter restores that inheritance to the appropriate people by solving the case.[19] The context in which Sayers surrounds the case, however, raises a number of problems that are not resolved at the conclusion of the novel.

The events of this novel are permeated by the realities of the aftermath of the Great War. The novel begins on Armistice Day, which commemorates the end of World War I. The body is found at a club established for war veterans, named the Bellona Club in honor of the Roman goddess of war. George, one of the key suspects in the murder, still suffers physically and psychologically from his time in the trenches. Early in the novel, he vividly expresses his frustration with these challenges when Peter asks him how he is doing:

> Oh, rotten as usual. Tummy all wrong and no money. What's the damn good of it, Wimsey? A man goes and fights for his country, gets his inside gassed out, and loses his job, and all they give him is the privilege of marching past the Cenotaph once a year and paying four shillings in the pound income-tax. Sheila's queer too—overwork, poor girl. It's pretty damnable for a man to have to live on his wife's earnings, isn't it? I can't help it, Wimsey. I go sick and have to chuck jobs up. Money—I never thought of money before the War, but I swear nowadays I'd commit any damned crime to get hold of a decent income.[20]

---

[19] Dorothy L. Sayers, *The Unpleasantness at the Bellona Club* (New York: Harper, 1995).
[20] *UBC*, 2.

With her description of George's plight, Sayers does much more than simply provide a motive for one of the suspects. She also highlights a situation that was true for many veterans who found it difficult to integrate back into society after the war. Even her own detective suffers from his time in the war; in *Whose Body?*, Sayers reveals that Peter continues to have nightmares about his experiences in the trenches. As Stacy Gillis recounts, "Ten years after the armistice, 2.5 million men were in receipt of a pension for some sort of war disability and forty-eight hospitals were tending 65,000 shell-shocked patients."[21] Many were still suffering, and this reality becomes a powerful background for the murder in *The Unpleasantness at the Bellona Club*.

Sayers emphasizes this context even further with the rather tasteless joke that George tells at the beginning of the novel. After complaining about the Bellona Club and comparing it to a morgue, George declares, "Place always reminds me of that old thing in 'Punch,' you know— 'Waiter, take away Lord Whatsisname, he's been dead two days.'"[22] The joke relies on the seemingly ridiculous idea that a community of people would fail to notice a corpse in their midst. But it is this idea that Sayers uses as the foundation for her mystery, for a few moments after the joke is told Peter discovers that George's grandfather, who has been sitting by the fire for several hours, is actually dead, a fact neither George nor anyone else in the club has noticed. For George, this discovery encapsulates precisely what he feels is wrong with the world after the war. He responds by becoming hysterical and crying, "Take him away! . . . Take him away. He's been dead two days! So are you! So

---

[21]Stacy Gillis, "Consoling Fictions: Mourning, World War One, and Dorothy L. Sayers," in *Modernism and Mourning*, ed. Patricia Rae (Lewisburg, PA: Bucknell University Press, 2007), 188.
[22]*UBC*, 1.

am I! We're all dead and we never noticed it."[23] While Sayers eventually grants George a happy ending with him "getting on splendidly" after the stress of the investigation,[24] the resonance of the joke and George's reaction to his grandfather's death continues. As Robert Kuhn McGregor and Ethan Lewis argue, "By weaving the most painful of sentiments into the text, by drawing fully rounded portraits of human beings still suffering from their wounds, Sayers gave her readers an opportunity to genuinely contemplate a long-forbidden subject."[25] While the mystery has been solved and many of the characters are recovering, the society that exists at the end of this novel is not entirely peaceful. It remains horribly damaged as a result of the war, a reality Sayers's original readers would have clearly understood.

Sayers challenges the simplistic view of society as generally peaceful and innocent even further in *Murder Must Advertise* (1933).[26] Here, Peter infiltrates the world of advertising and the drug culture surrounding a group of privileged socialites called the Bright Young People to discover the truth about a suspicious death. Thomas Michael Stein highlights the significance of Sayers's choices in this story, remarking, "What, in this novel, starts as a conventional murder investigation gradually develops into a complex and dedicated treatise on the exploitation of society."[27] In this novel, the community threatened with evil is an advertising agency, a world that Sayers knew well since she worked as a copywriter for S. H. Benson's from 1922 to 1930 and helped develop successful campaigns for Guinness and Colman's Mustard, among other

---

[23]*UBC*, 5.
[24]*UBC*, 240.
[25]Robert Kuhn McGregor with Ethan Lewis, *Conundrums for the Long Week-End: England, Dorothy L. Sayers, and Lord Peter Wimsey* (Kent, OH: Kent University Press, 2000), 73.
[26]Dorothy L. Sayers, *Murder Must Advertise* (New York: Harper, 1995).
[27]Thomas Michael Stein, "The Social Vision in Dorothy L. Sayers's Detective Fiction." *Inklings: Jahrbuch für Literatur und Ästhetik*, 12 (1994): 113.

clients. While Sayers reportedly enjoyed her job, in the novel she emphasizes how flawed this community can be both in the relationships that the workers have with each other and in the work that they do.

After one of the copywriters is killed by a seemingly innocent fall down the firm's iron staircase, Mr. Pym, the managing director, receives a letter from the deceased warning him about "something of a fishy nature" going on at the agency.[28] This prompts Mr. Pym to ask Peter to go undercover as a copywriter and see what he can discover. As Sayers recounts Peter's experiences, she shows him enjoying the casual camaraderie of the office as employees "worked happily together, writing each other's headlines in a helpful spirit and invading each other's rooms at all hours of the day."[29] But she also points to a darker side of this community, with its jealousies and rivalries that frequently divide the office into opposing camps. As Peter eventually discovers, "The spiritual atmosphere was clamorous with financial storm, intrigue, dissension, indigestion and marital infidelity. And with worse things—with murder wholesale and retail, of soul and body, murder by weapon and by poison."[30] In this community, it is no surprise that the copywriter's fall down the stairs proves to be a murder rather than an accidental death.

The problems with the advertising agency go even further than that, however, as Sayers repeatedly questions the work that these advertisers are doing and the effects it has on the wider society. Peter, for instance, describes advertising to Inspector Parker as "tell[ing] plausible lies for money" and declares, "Truth in advertising . . . is like leaven, which a woman hid in three measures of meal. It provides a suitable quantity

---

[28] *MMA*, 76.
[29] *MMA*, 34.
[30] *MMA*, 293.

of gas, with which to blow out a mass of crude misrepresentation into a form that the public can swallow."[31] He takes his critique even further later in the novel when he worries about the way advertising preys on "those who, aching for a luxury beyond their reach and for a leisure for ever [sic] denied them, could be bullied or wheedled into spending their few hardly won shillings on whatever might give them, if only for a moment, a leisured and luxurious illusion."[32] Rather than revealing an innocent world that must be purged of the evil that threatens it, Sayers emphasizes the dysfunction within this community while also questioning the very work that the advertisers do—and its negative effects on society. This critique becomes even more pointed when in the novel she intertwines the world of advertising with the drug culture of the Bright Young People.

With her characterization of the Bright Young People, Sayers references an actual group that came together in the years following World War I. As the biographer D. J. Taylor describes them, the Bright Young People of 1920s London were "a compound of cocktails, jazz, licence, abandon and flagrantly improper behavior."[33] They established an exclusive social scene, becoming known for their wild parties and silly antics. Today many see this group's behavior as a reaction to their growing up during the war. Taylor, for instance, remarks that "beneath the surface hubbub lay . . . a deep strain of unease, often extending to outright melancholy. Raised in the shadow of the Great War, denied most of the social and economic certainties of their parents' generation, the Bright Young People knew . . . that their pleasures came at

---

[31] *MMA*, 76.
[32] *MMA*, 188.
[33] D. J. Taylor, *Bright Young People: The Lost Generation of London's Jazz Age* (New York: Farrar, Straus and Giroux, 2007), 6.

a price, that somewhere in the middle distance a reckoning awaited."[34] Sayers's portrayal of the group, and particularly its leader Dian de Momerie, reveals a keen understanding of the desperation that fueled their escapades. Through these characters she builds on the social critique that she presented in *The Unpleasantness at the Bellona Club*, exploring another element of society that has been damaged as a result of the war. For example, Sayers captures Dian's mental state as she dances at one of the group's scandalous parties: "My God! I'm bored . . . Get off my feet, you clumsy cow . . . Money, tons of money . . . but I'm bored . . . Can't we do something else? . . . I'm sick of that tune . . . I'm sick of everything."[35] On the surface, the group appears to live an exciting, carefree life, but Sayers demonstrates that, at the core, their actions are fueled by a debilitating sense of emptiness.

While Sayers vividly reveals this desperation, she does not ultimately ask her readers to sympathize with the members of this group, for their decision to find solace in cocaine has serious repercussions not simply for them but also for the rest of society. After infiltrating one of their parties, Peter remarks, "There was enough dope floating about that house to poison a city."[36] The deaths of so many associated with the group suggest that his statement is not hyperbole. But the problem goes even further than this, for as one of the other characters reflects, "The worst of that crowd . . . is that they can't rest till they've made everybody they have to do with as bad as themselves. . . . They get hold of quite decent people and ruin them for life."[37] Thus for Sayers, the Bright Young People are not innocent victims crushed by the challenges of living in a post-war society; they are instead actively

---

[34]Taylor, *Bright Young People*, 12.
[35]*MMA*, 90.
[36]*MMA*, 85.
[37]*MMA*, 234.

pursuing the destruction of that society by entering into the drug trade and making a fortune off the desperation of others. They, like the advertisers, offer the illusion of luxury, glamour, and excitement for those who wish to escape the boring realities of their mundane lives.

Sayers makes this connection directly several times throughout the novel. Not only is the drug trade being carried out through messages hidden in the ads, but Peter also repeatedly reflects on the illusions that are being cultivated in both worlds and even uses that fascination with illusion to infiltrate the Bright Young People. By dressing up as a Harlequin, climbing to the top of a high fountain, and diving in, Peter immediately catches Dian's attention, for he creates a new illusion that breaks her out of her boredom. As he describes this rather bizarre choice to Inspector Parker, he remarks, "It pays to advertise,"[38] and later he responds to Dian's question about his peculiar behavior by stating, "Advertisement, chiefly. One must be different. . . . You may say it is a cheap way of producing an effect, and so it is; but it is good enough for gin-soaked minds."[39] Peter's success at using this personal form of advertising to infiltrate the group is then echoed at the end of the novel with the successful campaign for Wifflet cigarettes that he creates while posing as a copywriter. After uncovering the murderer and providing the police with the information they need to capture the leaders of the drug trade, Peter sees the first posters for his campaign going up around the city: "The great campaign had begun. He contemplated his work with a kind of amazement. With a few idle words on a sheet of paper he had touched the lives of millions."[40] The advertising campaign is based entirely on

---

[38] *MMA*, 87.
[39] *MMA*, 154.
[40] *MMA*, 355-56.

consumers purchasing cigarettes so they can collect coupons entitling them to free travel and lodging, or even a new house and furniture. Peter thus capitalizes on the dissatisfaction that characterizes not only the lives of the Bright Young People but also the lives of the everyday worker in Britain. Everyone is dissatisfied. The only difference among them is how they choose to appease their longings for something better.

Significantly, the conclusion of this novel does not return the reader to a peaceful, innocent world that has been purged of evil. Instead, Sayers concludes by emphasizing that the essential problems of society that were manifested so vividly in the Bright Young People still exist. While most people do not display their dissatisfaction so ostentatiously as the Bright Young People, they still experience it, and Sayers highlights this fact by concluding her novel with a paragraph composed entirely of advertising slogans:

> Tell England. Tell the world. Eat more Oats. Take Care of your Complexion. No More War. Shine your Shoes with Shino. Ask your Grocer. Children Love Laxamalt. Prepare to meet thy God. Bung's Beer is Better. Try Dogsbody Sausages. Whoosh the Dust Away. Give them Crunchlets. Snagsbury's Soups are Best for the Troops. *Morning Star*, best Paper by Far. Vote for Punkin and Protect your Profits. Stop that Sneeze with Snuffo. Flush your Kidneys with Fizzlets. Flush your Drains with Sanfect. Wear Wool-fleece next the Skin. Popp's Pills Pep you Up. Whiffle your Way to Fortune. . . . Advertise, or go under.[41]

While not all the slogans play on the public's dissatisfaction with their lives, Sayers ends with two that clearly do: one for Popp's Pills that chemically alter the consumer's mood, and one for Wifflet cigarettes

---

[41] *MMA*, 356.

that plays on consumers' desires for a more glamorous life. The murder may have been solved, and the drug trade may have been hampered by the discovery of the perpetrators, but the underlying feelings of emptiness and dissatisfaction remain in this society.

With both *The Unpleasantness at the Bellona Club* and *Murder Must Advertise* Sayers subverts the traditional formula of the detective novel. Rather than presenting comforting endings in which the detective both solves the case and also resolves the problems that threaten the community, Sayers illustrates that there are essential problems in the worlds of these novels that transcend the detective's power. And the fact that the worlds of these novels so closely mirror the world of Britain in the late 1920s and early 1930s, when the novels were written, suggests that Sayers is also asking her readers to move beyond these fictional realities to the challenges facing their own world. But if the detective cannot solve all these problems, who can? Sayers explores this question, gradually asking her readers to rethink the role of the detective as they follow Peter's career through her various novels. Just as she begins to break away from the traditional representations of innocent community, she also begins to challenge the image of the lone, brilliant detective.

Rethinking the Role of the Detective

Throughout her novels, Sayers repeatedly invokes Sherlock Holmes, the quintessential example of the lone, brilliant detective, and she makes clear connections between him and Peter. But even from the beginning, Sayers reveals that Peter does not quite fit the stereotype, and as she begins to develop Peter more fully as a character, she not only challenges this convention but also begins to suggest a better way to address the challenges of society. In *Whose Body?*, Sayers begins her treatment of Peter's career by establishing a clear connection between him and Sherlock Holmes. When Peter's mother calls and tells him that "a respectable Battersea architect has discovered a dead man in his bath,"[42] Peter springs into action, sending his servant Bunter off to an auction in his place to bid for some fifteenth-century editions of various literary works so that he can focus on solving the intriguing mystery. As Peter goes to change his clothes, he declares, "Exit the amateur of first editions; . . . enter Sherlock Holmes, disguised as a walking gentleman."[43] The fact that he then proceeds to supply himself with a monocle, which is also a powerful magnifying glass; a walking stick, which serves as a measuring rod as well as a weapon; and "a flat silver matchbox,"[44] which is also a tiny flashlight, suggests that he is fully prepared, as Holmes always is, to face any difficulties by himself.

As the story progresses, however, we soon realize that Peter does not solve the case by himself. He needs the help of both Bunter and Inspector Parker, both of whom are much more active in detective work than Watson ever is. Bunter is in charge of photographing the evidence and looking for the clues that the pictures reveal, and Parker does much of the leg work, a fact that he himself draws attention to. When Peter asks for Parker's advice on his case, which seems strangely connected to a case Parker is working on, Parker declares, "I'd do some good, hard grind. . . . I'd distrust every bit of work Sugg [another police officer] ever did, and I'd get the family history of every tenant of every flat in Queen Caroline Mansions. I'd examine all their box-rooms and roof-traps, and I would inveigle them into conversations."[45] Upon Peter responding, "You would, would you? . . . Well, we've exchanged cases, you know, so just you toddle off and do it," Parker "grimace[s]"

---

[42]*WB*, 4.
[43]*WB*, 5.
[44]*WB*, 6.
[45]*WB*, 56.

and says, "I don't suppose you'd ever do it, so I'd better."[46] As McGregor and Lewis point out, "Charles Parker is not Conan Doyle's Doctor Watson nor his Inspector LeStrade. He and Wimsey are genuinely a team. Parker—steady, plodding, but very intelligent—is capable of performing the grinding police work that Wimsey cannot."[47] But even beyond this, Parker occasionally acts as Peter's conscience, for he is the one who warns Peter that he cannot treat detection simply as a game where he "hunt[s] down a murderer for the sport of the thing and then shake[s] hands with him and say[s], 'Well played—hard luck—you shall have your revenge tomorrow!'"[48] By reminding Peter that he is "a responsible person," Parker compels him to acknowledge that he cannot separate the "game" of detection from the immorality of murder.[49] Ultimately, Peter solves the case in a manner worthy of Holmes, for as he sits home alone with "his pipe in his mouth and [the] jazz-coloured peacocks [on his dressing gown] gathered about him," he has a sudden moment of insight where all the clues miraculously come together in his mind.[50] In order to reach this point, however, he needs the help of Parker and Bunter, and he needs them much more than Holmes ever needs Watson.

In her later novels, Sayers develops this idea even further as she increases the number of friends who help Peter solve his cases, eventually demonstrating that the problems of society might be addressed more effectively by a community of individuals actively pursuing their unique vocations. She does this most fully in her novel *Strong Poison* (1930).[51] Here Peter must draw on a whole host of friends, who use

---

[46]*WB*, 56.
[47]McGregor and Lewis, *Conundrums*, 36-37.
[48]*WB*, 129-30.
[49]*WB*, 130.
[50]*WB*, 134.
[51]Dorothy L. Sayers, *Strong Poison* (New York: Harper, 1995).

their particular skills to prove the innocence of Harriet Vane, the woman with whom he has fallen in love and who is facing execution for the murder of Philip Boyes, her former lover. Because of his love for Harriet, Peter has difficulty grappling with this case. Early in the novel, the narrator recounts Peter's frustrations:

> For the first time... he doubted his own power to carry through what he had undertaken. His personal feelings had been involved before this in his investigations, but they had never before clouded his mind. He was fumbling—grasping uncertainly here and there at fugitive and mocking possibilities. He asked questions at random, doubtful of his object, and the shortness of the time, which would once have stimulated, now frightened and confused him.[52]

Amid his confusion, Peter needs the help of a fairly wide community of friends to solve the mystery. While Peter does do some of the legwork for this case, he is surprisingly inactive for much of the novel, relying on his friends to use their specific talents and resources to discover the necessary clues.

In fact, the first stop in his investigation is Scotland Yard, where he meets with Inspector Parker and declares, "For God's sake, old man, do what you can to put the thing right before next assizes [court session]."[53] Peter needs the police to go back over the evidence and make sure that they have correctly traced Boyes's movements on the night of his death. He also needs Bunter to work his magic with the cook and the parlor maid in the house where Boyes died. Peter asks him, "Do you feel at your brightest and most truly fascinating? ...

---

[52]*SP*, 90.
[53]*SP*, 55-56.

Have you got that sort of conquering feeling? The Don Juan touch, so to speak?"[54] Peter needs to make sure he has all the details surrounding Boyes's final meal, and Bunter, with his ability to charm the female servants, has a much better chance of getting that information than Peter does. And even when Peter himself is doing the investigating, he needs his friends to help him get access to the right information. For example, he asks Marjorie Phelps, an artist, to introduce him to the Bohemian world of London that Boyes frequented, and he calls on Freddy Arbuthnot, a financial expert, to investigate the investments of Boyes's cousin. Unlike the stereotypical lone detective who is able to easily infiltrate any community and discover all the necessary clues without much outside help, Peter repeatedly relies on his friends to do the work that they are more qualified to do.

Sayers emphasizes this notion even more particularly when Peter calls upon an establishment that he has nicknamed the "Cattery" to help him with the investigation. On the surface, the Cattery is simply a pool of female typists. But it is actually a private investigation bureau financed by Peter but run by Miss Katherine Climpson, a middle-aged spinster who helped Peter investigate a murder in the earlier novel *Unnatural Death*. In that novel, Peter describes Miss Climpson as "a manifestation of the wasteful way in which this country is run" and then explains this waste to Inspector Parker:

> Thousands of old maids, simply bursting with useful energy, forced by our stupid social system into hydros and hotels and communities and hostels and posts as companions, where their magnificent gossip-powers and units of inquisitiveness are allowed to dissipate themselves or even become harmful to the

---
[54]*SP*, 77.

community, while the rate-payers' money is spent on getting work for which these women are providentially fitted, inefficiently carried out by ill-equipped policemen like you.[55]

With the Cattery, Peter has harnessed this useful energy, and in *Strong Poison* he utilizes these women's particular skills to help him gather the clues he needs to solve the case.

Perhaps surprisingly, the most interesting detective work that occurs in *Strong Poison* is not done by Peter but rather by two women from the Cattery: Miss Murchison and Miss Climpson. Miss Murchison infiltrates the law office of Boyes's cousin, Mr. Urquhart, as a secretary, and with a little help from Mr. Rumm, another of Peter's friends, she learns how to pick locks so that she can investigate Mr. Urquhart's paperwork pertaining to the will of Mr. Boyes's aunt. Miss Climpson does even more work, for she must gain access to the original will and ensure that it is sent to Urquhart's office for Miss Murchison to find and copy. Miss Climpson must therefore travel to the town where the aunt lies on the verge of death, develop a friendship with the nurse who is caring for her, and somehow convince the nurse to break into the safe, get the will, and send it to the lawyer—a feat Miss Climpson accomplishes by masterfully faking a séance.

Before visiting Miss Climpson and asking for her help, Peter is quite literally at his wit's end, reflecting on his inability to solve the case as he looks at the books on his shelves:

> All that wisdom and all that beauty, and they could not show him how to save the woman he imperiously wanted from a sordid death by hanging. And he had thought himself rather clever at

---

[55]Dorothy L. Sayers, *Unnatural Death* (New York: Harper, 1995), 28.

that kind of thing. The enormous and complicated imbecility of things was all round him like a trap. He ground his teeth and raged helplessly, striding about the suave, wealthy, futile room.[56]

With all his knowledge and wealth, Peter cannot solve this case on his own. As McGregor and Lewis remark, "Peter is unusually helpless in *Strong Poison*. . . . Peter can only stand and wait, an endless agony of waiting for the others to do what is necessary."[57] He needs Inspector Parker, Bunter, Marjorie, Freddy, Mr. Rumm, and Miss Murchison to help him discover and access the clues, and even after all that help, he still needs Miss Climpson's particular skills as an investigator to provide the final piece of evidence.

Near the end of the novel, Peter does have his Sherlock Holmes moment as he tells Parker, "Give me the statutory dressing-gown and an ounce of shag [tobacco], and I will undertake to dispose of this little difficulty for you in a brace of shakes."[58] He and his friends have collected all the clues, but Peter needs to figure out one remaining element: how the poison was administered. And after a night alone, he does so. This moment is overshadowed, however, by all the help Peter received in this case. While ultimately he pulls all the information together, he needs everyone else's evidence to make a compelling argument, a fact that he acknowledges to Parker, declaring, "You will no doubt take steps to secure, in an official and laborious manner, the evidence which our kind friends here have already so ably gathered in by unconventional methods, and will stand by to arrest the right man when the time comes."[59] Thus, by the end of the

---

[56]*SP*, 168.
[57]McGregor and Lewis, *Conundrums*, 95.
[58]*SP*, 242.
[59]*SP*, 242.

novel, Sayers has masterfully shifted the focus from the individual detective to the community that surrounds him, a community that supports his job by doing their own work extremely well. She also implicitly broadens this vision by demonstrating that Inspector Parker, Miss Climpson, and Miss Murchison are not simply waiting around until they can be useful to Peter. They are actively pursuing their own vocations and doing their own work to make their community better. Parker, of course, has other cases, and the women of the Cattery are busy discovering "fraud, blackmail or attempted procuration" in newspaper advertisements and passing on information to the police.[60] The world at the end of *Strong Poison* may be just as flawed as the worlds at the end of *The Unpleasantness at the Bellona Club* and *Murder Must Advertise*, but here Sayers demonstrates—through the work of Peter's friends at Scotland Yard and the Cattery—that others (besides the individual detective) are busy doing their part to repair society.

As we can see when contrasting her later novels with her earlier ones, Sayers, by moving beyond traditional conventions, has deepened the artistry of her works and created a more realistic view of evil and a more complex view of the (limited) power of the detective. Through the complexities of *The Unpleasantness at the Bellona Club*, *Murder Must Advertise*, and *Strong Poison*, Sayers compels her readers to reflect much more deeply on issues of community than they are able to do when reading the simpler mysteries of *Whose Body?* and *Clouds of Witness*. And as she deepens her artistry, she also presents a powerful image of the type of ideal community that she would later discuss in more explicitly theological terms in *The Mind of the Maker* and "Why Work?"

---

[60]*SP*, 50.

The Important Role of Individual Action in Community

Today, we tend to think of *The Mind of the Maker* primarily as a fascinating exploration of the Trinity, for Sayers uses the analogy of the creative mind to help her readers understand the ways that God the Father, Son, and Spirit interact in relationship. However, Sayers was attempting to do much more with this work. Published in 1941 during World War II, *The Mind of the Maker* is also a response to the realities of that war, realities that Sayers had earlier (in *Begin Here*) related directly to a false conception of community. In *The Mind of the Maker* Sayers builds on her ideas in *Begin Here* and attempts to help her readers understand God's purposes both for individuals and for society. The core of her argument is that "the Trinitarian structure which can be shown to exist in the mind of man and in all his works is, in fact, the integral structure of the universe, and corresponds . . . with the nature of God, in Whom all that is exists."[61] Even more specifically, Sayers contends that the "creative mind is in fact the very grain of the spiritual universe" and is therefore "exhibited in the spiritual structure of every man and woman."[62] Sayers believes that God has created each individual with a unique creative mind that mirrors the trinitarian structure of the Godhead. She then uses that foundation to argue, first, that society has fallen apart because people have ignored this fundamental truth and, second, that true community will be restored only when individuals fully engage their creative minds and embrace the unique work God designed them to do. For Sayers, this type of work is both "a sacrament and manifestation of man's creative energy,"[63] and

---

[61]Sayers, *Mind of the Maker*, xiii.
[62]Sayers, *Mind of the Maker*, 185.
[63]Sayers, *Mind of the Maker*, 218.

she believes that God ultimately uses it to preserve the essential balance between the needs of the individual and the health of the community.

Sayers develops these ideas more directly in her essay "Why Work?" (1942), and it is here that we see even more clearly the connection between work and community that she had already been exploring in her detective fiction. For Sayers, work is intensely personal. It should be not only "the work for which [the worker] is fitted by nature"[64] but also "the full expression of the worker's faculties, the thing in which he finds spiritual, mental, and bodily satisfaction, and the medium in which he offers himself to God."[65] Therefore, it is only by aligning our creative minds with the work God has created us to do that we will ever find true satisfaction. This is also, according to Sayers, the only way to establish and preserve true community. She asserts that "the only way to serve the community is to forget the community and serve the work."[66] The underlying assumption here is that if individuals faithfully channel their creative energy into their proper work, God will ultimately combine each individual's work with the work of others in perfect harmony so that the overall community functions effectively.

Sayers, perhaps surprisingly, does not explicitly address God's role in preserving the community's health in "Why Work?" For a clearer expression of this idea, we must return to *The Nine Tailors*, the detective novel with which I began. Toward the end of that novel, Peter struggles with the idea that by doing his proper work as a detective he may be hurting the community rather than helping it. He complains, "I rather wish I hadn't come buttin' into this. Some things may be better

---

[64]Dorothy L. Sayers, "Why Work?" in *Creed or Chaos*? (London: Methuen & Co. Ltd., 1947), 56.
[65]Sayers, "Why Work?," 55.
[66]Sayers, "Why Work?," 62.

left alone, don't you think?"⁶⁷ In response, Mr. Venables, the minister of the small community where the crime took place, declares, "My dear boy ... it does not do for us to take too much thought for the morrow. It is better to follow the truth and leave the result in the hand of God. He can foresee where we cannot, because He knows all the facts."⁶⁸ Earlier in the story, Peter had compared his frustrations with figuring out the mystery to the complexities of change ringing, complaining that his bell was "lying behind the whole way."⁶⁹ It is thus significant that Venables, both a minister and an avid change ringer, is the one who reminds Peter of the need to trust in God's knowledge of the whole picture. As a change ringer, Venables has been trained to listen for the order that lies behind the seeming confusion of the bells, and as a faithful minister, he is confident that God's order ultimately governs real life even when humans cannot perceive it. As Sayers portrays throughout her works, living well in community is a much more "intricate ritual" than even the complex art of change ringing, and at times, we may not understand how our particular work fits with the work of others to create the beautifully complex order of society. Unlike expert change ringers, we cannot always hear the order that exists behind the "monotonous jangle"⁷⁰ of individuals doing the work they are called to do. But Sayers, like Venables, seems confident that if we focus on serving God through the proper work for which he has designed us, he will ultimately bring order to the community.

In response to the realities of World War II, Sayers began to reflect more theologically on both work and community. She acknowledges that "it may well seem ... that I have a sort of obsession about this

---

⁶⁷*NT*, 306.
⁶⁸*NT*, 307.
⁶⁹*NT*, 282.
⁷⁰*NT*, 22.

business of the right attitude to work. But I do insist upon it, because it seems to me that what becomes of civilization after this war is going to depend enormously on our being able to effect this revolution in our ideas about work."[71] This obsession was, in fact, one that she had already been developing in her detective fiction, for as she began to explore the evils of society in more complex ways, she also began to realize that these evils demanded a more complex solution than the one usually created by detective writers.

Sayers did not write her detective fiction intending to present a theological perspective on community. But as an artist trying to do her proper work with integrity, she began to recognize that preserving the complex communities she was beginning to create within her novels required more than simply the brilliance of Lord Peter Wimsey. It required Miss Climpson's insights into human nature and her ability to fake a séance just as much as it required Inspector Parker's plodding police work, Freddie Arbuthnot's knowledge of the stock market, Marjorie Phelps's insight into the artistic mind, and Miss Murchison's secretarial skills. By focusing on their unique work and taking action when needed, they all ended up serving the wider community. Their skills came together with everyone else's, ultimately providing a powerful model of the balance between individuals and community that Sayers hoped would help transform her own society.

---

[71]Sayers, "Why Work?," 47.

RESPONSE

Tiffany Eberle Kriner

When Dorothy Sayers's character Harriet Vane writes a mystery novel, Vane's sleuth-hero, Robert Templeton, solves the mystery using a two-columned list: *Things to Be Noted* and *Things to Be Done*. Under *Things to Be Noted* go the facts. Under *Things to Be Done* go tasks that respond to the facts. That's a fair outline of how I will proceed here.

First, the facts of the case that Colón has set forth, the *Things to Be Noted*:

1. Colón has argued that over the course of Dorothy Sayers's career in writing detective fiction, Sayers develops a theology of active community. According to this theology, humans should live out their vocation by fully engaging their creative selves (mind, soul, and body) and embracing their unique work. If they do so in peace and collaboration with others, true community will emerge in which humans can participate in providentially ordained restoration of this broken world.

2. Colón has shown Sayers's development of this theology within increasingly realistic uses of the elements of detective fiction.

    a. Through her early work, Sayers learned to redeploy stock genre requirements of detective fiction. The communities in which the crimes take place, often stock peaceful settings, are shown as persistently and complexly corrupt—as places of recalcitrant, wicked problems. In redeploying the stock genre requirements, Sayers engages the reading audience with more complex problems, giving them responsibility to act.

b. Sayers's maturing craft manifests in more realistic detective characters, whom she invests with more nuance than the brilliant but mostly predictable Sherlock Holmes. Instead of being able to step in and save the day, characters such as Peter Wimsey and Harriet Vane learn that solving even a piece of many of the problems requires a community, each member of which contributes their unique gifts.

These points, I believe, are the *Things to Be Noted*.

My response will offer *Things to Be Done*. I'd like to focus on the way that two particularly realistic features of detective fiction (at least, as practiced by Sayers), namely *setting* and *corpses*, give us some lessons in building and/or joining a community of action as developed by Sayers and illuminated by Colón. The book that will illustrate these lessons comes from within the time period Colón has covered in her essay, when both Sayers and her characters were developing more realistic engagements with the problems of this world. *Have His Carcase* (1932) is the second novel in which Harriet Vane appears as a partner-in-crime-fighting to Peter Wimsey—and also as a potential life partner. In the novel, Harriet, broken in spirit by both the public humiliation of having been tried for murder and the ongoing private humiliation of being indebted to Peter Wimsey for clearing her name, escapes it all on a walking tour of the southwest coast of England. One June day, at low tide, she discovers a body on a rock near a seaside resort town.

Now, it may seem suspect for me to use a literary-studies type reading of this detective novel to give us some ways to operationalize the theology of community we've just read about. It is perhaps odd. But I take Harriet Vane's words as warrant—or at least as precedent. In

Have His Carcase, when the police inspector commends her level-headed actions upon encountering the corpse, she says, "I know what ought to be done. I write detective stories, you know."[1] Perhaps we may can know what needs to be done to enact Sayers's theology of community by *reading* her detective story.

Reading *Have His Carcase*, we find that the first thing to be done, then, to solve the wicked problems of the world is to *pay attention to place*, because the landscape and environment—both the natural world and the social world—register the complex problems to which we must apply our full creative gifts. By focusing us outside ourselves, place gives us a first cue for how to recognize the existence and the gifts of others. We see this working out by briefly looking at setting in the novel. Scholars have remarked that the reader is "never too far from the geographical milieu," but Sayers often reveals her characters' states and relationships with the community through the actual setting itself.[2] In the opening of *Have His Carcase*, for instance, the landscape, described above all as solitary, reflects the desire for escape from public and private shame. Sayers's use of free, indirect style suggests Harriet sees the landscape in ways that suit *her* purpose. Harriet uses the landscape, following "a steady course" to a town that's described as a "convenient objective" for solitude.[3] The opening description is liberally dosed with the refrain "here and there." The beach is "broken here and there by scattered rocks, which rose successively . . . from the reluctant and withdrawing tide."[4] The sky is "fretted here and there with faint white clouds."[5] A shepherd passes "here and there" with a dog "alike

---

[1] Dorothy L. Sayers, *Have His Carcase* (New York: Harper & Row, 1960), 106.
[2] Douglas R. McManis, "Places for Mysteries," *Geographical Review* 68, no. 3 (July 1978): 329, www.jstor.org/stable/215050.
[3] *HHC*, 7, 8.
[4] *HHC*, 9.
[5] *HHC*, 9.

indifferent and preoccupied." "Here and there" shy horses look at her.[6] And there are more. These features of the landscape are described as replicable and more or less interchangeable. The animals are looking at her (rather than she at them) and greet her "with heavy snufflings" (rather than she greeting them).[7] Harriet isn't looking at the place, and she isn't doing her work. Nor is there a sense of community.

Only when Harriet begins to play detective storywriter, trying to puzzle out how the tides actually work as she stops for lunch—when she is actually looking carefully at the place as more than a background for her own intention—does she see the true problems that inhere in the landscape itself (which in this story are primarily tied to the body). For Sayers, in this book the problem of the murder is a problem of the landscape as much as anything: the body is described as a feature of the landscape. Harriet thinks, "Is that rock covered at high tide? Yes, of course. . . . How odd that it should have seaweed only in that lump at the top. . . . It's very peculiar. It looks almost more like a man lying down; is it possible for seaweed to be so very—well, so very localised?"[8] Yes, it turns out, because the seaweed is a dead body, and inherent in the landscape is a problem—murder—that eventually touches all the creatures and spaces represented heretofore as "here and there." Both the wickedness of the problem and the worked-out analysis of problem and solution require attentiveness to place.

My point here is to connect the novel's impulses about detectives and settings to our own *Things to Be Done* to develop communities of action. In *Have His Carcase,* Peter and Harriet, as detectives, need to be localized in the place where they wish to solve the problem, getting

---

[6]*HHC*, 9.
[7]*HHC*, 9.
[8]*HHC*, 11.

to know the people and the landscape. Peter and Harriet have to go swimming in the freezing cold water with tricky tides to find a key clue. They have to comb the beach for hours, picking trash, to find a lucky horseshoe clue. Harriet has to actually move in to the deceased's former living quarters, reading the dead man's books and using his dictionary, to figure out how the murder has been committed—and why. They are unable to learn anything on a simple walk or drive through the area but must return to the places again and again to understand the problem and try to solve it. And in their learning of landscape, they experience the extent to which nature itself, along with the human community members, offers its gifts to the project. When Harriet first discovers the body, she is in great distress and tries to call out to a fishing boat far out in the water—one of those "here and there" objects from earlier. Here's what the text says at this point: "As she stood, hopelessly calling, she felt a wet touch on her foot. The tide had undoubtedly turned, and was coming in fast. Quite suddenly, this fact registered itself in her mind and seemed to clear her brain completely."[9] The landscape—here the sea—which had been considered withdrawing and distant, reached out almost as if in response to her call. Sayers thus portrays the landscape as giving Harriet Vane its own clue: the fact of the tides.

This attentiveness to place is utterly necessary for the solvers (and writers) of murder mysteries, who find or put vital information in the environment. I suspect it is also necessary, a *Thing to Be Done*, for members of theologically vital communities of action (that is, for us), in which members of the body of Christ seek to participate in the love of the Trinity toward the community of the new creation. Our theologies of incarnation and of eschatology suggest both that God has

---

[9] *HHC*, 15.

time and place for us and that God does not abandon his creation but makes it new. We may learn from settings in detective fiction what ought to be done: we must no longer view places as background to our "steady course[s]" or "convenient objective[s]."[10] No more just passing through. Paying attention to place is vital to finding the problem—to noting its persistence and complexity—and to helping, alongside all creation, to solve it.

The second *Thing to Be Done* to build communities of action to solve wicked problems emerges out of a particularly central convention of murder mysteries—that there is a corpse. The corpses of murder mysteries remind us that to build a community of action, we must *pay more attention to bodies*.

Sayers underscores in several ways the desperate need to attend to bodies. In *Have His Carcase*, not only does the title offer up the corpse as central, but for most of the novel, the corpse is, in fact, missing. Though Harriet photographs the body, it ends up being washed away by the incoming tide before the police can recover it. Sayers humorously highlights the point of the body's essentialness when Harriet and Peter do their own *Things to Be Noted / Things to Be Done* exercise. The *Thing to Be Noted* was, "He was found dead on the rock with his throat cut." This fact is opposed, under *Things to Be Done*, in all caps with a full stop: "FIND THE BODY."[11]

This absence of the body is the novel's funny, literal way of indicating a communal need for attentiveness to physical bodies and to embodied persons in their individuality. In the end, the physical body comes to be very important indeed to the solution of the mystery. But even before that, the body is more than just plot—moving toward

---
[10]*HHC*, 7, 8.
[11]*HHC*, 166.

theme and moving toward our *Things to Be Done*. When the body of Paul Alexis is recovered, we learn that his face—the site of recognition and identity—has been picked off by lobsters during his underwater sojourn. Sayers's blisteringly ironic description of the town's response to this news—merely to avoid serving lobster or crab at the resort for a fortnight—shows how they have refused to recognize or welcome him. In fact, the town basically refuses to attend to Alexis's body at all, except for how it serves their appetites or convenience or theatrics or will. He was a paid escort, and his gross death interrupts the entertainment—or gets refashioned as entertainment of another sort.

Almost everyone in the story except (and note this well!) the coroner, instead of attending to the particularities of his body or face or person, is very keen on noting and marking Alexis's body as blanket "other," both racially and politically. Racial slurs such as "dago" dog the talk of Alexis, though he is, in fact—as the coroner points out in the inquest—a naturalized British citizen of Russian descent. It is this Russian descent piece that works as a central marker of otherness for the town. One of the jury members uses the inquiry into the death to suggest that "with two million British born workers unemployed . . . it [was] a scandalous thing that this foreign riff-raff was allowed to land at all."[12] Even the inspector on the case assumes suicide because the character is Russian, and "he himself had read a great deal of Russian literature and could assure the jury that suicide was a frequent occurrence among the members of that unhappy nation."[13] They are not attending to bodies; they are marking bodies as cardboard cutouts, stereotypes, and stories.

For people in the town, and from a police standpoint, it would be better and simpler if Paul Alexis had killed himself (in which case he

---

[12]*HHC*, 279.
[13]*HHC*, 280.

could be easily dismissed as a sad case) or had never come into the community at all. His body, whether absent or present, is a disturbance once it is no longer of use. There are plenty of interchangeable paid escorts, as the mourning fiancée's quick change of love interest shows. Even though paying attention to bodies—of the victim and of the perpetrators—turns the case entirely and solves the mystery, Peter's suggestion that they exhume the body to note particular features relevant to the case is met with groans: "See here, my lord, if we do prosecute, d'you really think we've a hope in Hades?"[14] The end of the novel pictures Peter and Harriet leaving the town abruptly in disgust at the official response. They have not progressed in solving the wicked problems that led to Paul Alexis's death, even if they have solved the whodunnit.

This *Thing to Be Done*, attend to the bodies—that is, to embodied persons—is key for solving murder mysteries if you're Peter Wimsey, and to writing murder mysteries if you're Harriet Vane. But I'd like to suggest that for Sayers, it's also one of our *Things to Be Done* in order to live in communities of action that may have some hope of solving the wicked problems in our world. For a mystery writer like Dorothy Sayers, that meant pushing Peter Wimsey and Harriet Vane beyond the cardboard roles the genre offered, to make them more real. Colón showed us this was a goal of Sayers's—to move beyond the formulaic detective story to the novel of manners, namely, the novel of humanity. For us, we must remember that bodies matter in the life of faith—attending to them will underscore the ways in which the problems we'd like to pawn off on a single outlier form part of more wicked matrices.

We like to focus on what we can do, our own Sherlock Holmes contributions and deductions. But we must never forget bodies and our own implication in their suffering. We have reaped women and

---

[14]*HHC*, 488.

men for our own convenience and privilege and rest—and we must start with that fundamental fact telling. Remembering bodies can lead us to attend to the myriad persons who contribute to the community of action and the solutions. When characters in our communities play stock roles, are cardboard characters short-handed by us into categories of use or engagement, we disable such people from being involved in meaningful contributions to the solution. We can make others useless by not recognizing and welcoming their gifts.

I believe Christine Colón has helped build the community of action—she has done it—by treating Sayers's milieu with care to find its problems and complex processes. She has done it by noting Sayers's slow development toward a better detective novel that can contribute to the addressing of wicked problems. And she has done it by paying attention to the corpus of the work as a whole. If my deductions are correct and these points come together at all, then you can go and do it too.

DOROTHY L. SAYERS'S VISION FOR COMMUNITIES OF FAITH

*I*N 1936, DOROTHY SAYERS WAS ASKED to write a play for a festival at Canterbury Cathedral. As she considered subjects that she might explore, Sayers was drawn to the story of William of Sens, the architect who was commissioned to rebuild a section of Canterbury Cathedral after a devastating fire in 1174. Throughout the play, which Sayers entitled *The Zeal of Thy House*, she focuses on William as a master craftsman and emphasizes the detailed work involved in rebuilding the cathedral. In particular, she concentrates on the process of building the arches. Early in the play, William asks Hubert (his superintendent), "How about that new arch? D'you think she's settled in? I'd like to get those supports out to-day."¹ These questions then provoke a discussion about the beauties of a perfectly constructed arch. Hubert begins by reflecting on the words of a former mentor: "The arch is the secret of the building. We ain't half learned yet . . . what the arch can carry when it's put to it."² He then concludes with his own thoughts: "That's the way to build. Each stone carrying his neighbour's

---

¹Dorothy L. Sayers, *The Zeal of Thy House* (Eugene, OR: Wipf & Stock, 2011), 58.
²*ZH*, 58.

burden."³ William affirms Hubert's ideas, remarking, "A triumph of balance, eh, Hubert? A delicate adjustment of interlocking stresses."⁴

As Sayers recognizes, a well-built arch is truly a "triumph of balance." The builders must carefully position the stones around a support frame as they first craft the pillars and then build up to the actual arch. As they build, they must work with precision, for the placement of each stone is critical: each stone must be able to withstand the stresses of the others once the support is removed. Ultimately, the arch is held together by the capstone or keystone at the top of the arch, which is the final stone to be placed. This keystone, which is usually shaped like a wedge, locks all the other stones together, transferring the stresses of the arch from the support frame to the pillars and allowing it to stand once the support has been removed.⁵ A well-constructed arch, then, is truly "a delicate adjustment of interlocking stresses."

As we will soon see, an arch plays an important role in the plot of *The Zeal of Thy House*. But in addition to that, I believe the arch serves as a powerful symbol of Sayers's developing ideas about the components needed to maintain healthy communities of faith: committed individuals who are willing to participate in the work of bearing one another's burdens (like the stones in an arch) and a centering doctrine that acts like a keystone to hold those individuals together. With this essay, I would like to explore how these two ideas circulate throughout Sayers's religious plays as she grapples with the various challenges that threaten to weaken the stability of the church and destroy its influence on society.

In my first essay, I discussed the ways that Sayers's ideas about communities of action developed over the course of her detective novels

---

³*ZH*, 59.
⁴*ZH*, 59.
⁵For a good example of the process of building an arch, watch "Arch Construction Fast" on YouTube: www.youtu.be/Vdg-6_XheEo.

as she began to focus on the importance of individuals developing their own particular skills and joining with others in community so that those skills could be used together to help combat the evils of the world. I also suggested that with the development of her detective novels, Sayers set the stage for her later theological works, in which she addresses the challenges of helping society recover after the ravages of World War II. In her career as a religious playwright, to which she transitioned in the late 1930s just before the outbreak of the war, Sayers explores the complexities of community even more deeply, focusing particularly on Christian community. With these plays, she presents a number of difficulties faced by communities of faith as they attempt to be communities of action, and she reveals the components that she believes will help these communities be more effective. Significantly, it is at this point in her life that Sayers herself is initiated into a new community—the world of theater—which seemed to open her eyes even more fully to the power of individuals coming together to work toward a common goal. Through the experiences of creating and presenting her religious dramas, Sayers solidified her ideas about the key elements that are necessary to preserve communities of faith and allow them to be centers of action. And, interestingly, as she observes her own society, she finds that the best model for this type of healthy community is not in the contemporary church but rather in the theatrical communities that she worked with to create her plays.

DISINTEGRATION OF COMMUNITY

Before looking at how Sayers delineates these necessary elements for communities of faith in her plays, however, we must first see how Sayers describes the problems that have contributed to the disintegration of these communities in the first place. With the outbreak of

World War II, Sayers, along with many other Christian intellectuals, began to reflect on the ways that the supposedly Christian society of Great Britain might not be prepared for the challenges of the war. In "Creed or Chaos?," which was delivered as a lecture in 1940, Sayers characterizes the war as "a life-and-death struggle between Christian and pagan,"[6] and she declares that "at bottom it is a violent and irreconcilable quarrel about the nature of God and the nature of man and the ultimate nature of the universe."[7] Sayers contends that what is "terrifying and tremendous" about the war is that it is based not on a "failure in Germany to live up to her own standards of right conduct" but rather that "what we believe to be evil, Germany believes to be good."[8] For Sayers, the fundamental issue at stake in the war is the truth of Christianity. She is therefore adamant that those who claim to be Christians must be fully grounded in the doctrines they supposedly believe. In fact, Sayers implies that unless the people of Britain truly understand Christian doctrine, they run the risk of winning the battle against Germany but losing the war against paganism: a war they do not even realize they should be fighting.

For Sayers, this danger is a very real one. Not only does she believe that "not one person in a hundred has the faintest notion what the Church teaches about God or man or society or the person of Jesus Christ,"[9] but she also worries that even devout Christians, who should know better, are ignoring the importance of doctrine in a mistaken belief that it makes Christianity unappealing. She imagines them exclaiming, "Away with the tedious complexities of dogma—let us have

---

[6]Dorothy L. Sayers, "Creed or Chaos?" in *Creed or Chaos*? (London: Methuen & Co. Ltd., 1947), 25.
[7]Sayers, "Creed or Chaos?," 25.
[8]Sayers, "Creed or Chaos?," 26.
[9]Sayers, "Creed or Chaos?," 28.

Dorothy L. Sayers's Vision for Communities of Faith

the simple spirit of worship; just worship, no matter of what!"[10] Essentially, Sayers characterizes the Christians of Britain as trying to maintain the arch of Christian community without the keystone of doctrine, and throughout her works, she repeatedly demonstrates how ridiculous that is. In her essay "The Dogma Is the Drama," for instance, Sayers crafts an imaginary catechism that illustrates what Christians actually seem to believe:

Q: What does the Church think of God the Father?

A: He is omnipotent and holy. He created the world and imposed on man conditions impossible of fulfillment; He is very angry if these are not carried out. He sometimes interferes by means of arbitrary judgments and miracles, distributed with a good deal of favoritism. He likes to be truckled to and is always ready to pounce on anybody who trips up over a difficulty in the Law, or is having a bit of fun. He is rather like a dictator, only larger and more arbitrary.

Q: What does the Church think of God the Son?

A: He is in some way to be identified with Jesus of Nazareth. It was not His fault that the world was made like this, and, unlike God the Father, He is friendly to man and did His best to reconcile man to God (see *Atonement*). He has a good deal of influence with God, and if you want anything done, it is best to apply to Him.

Q: What does the Church think about God the Holy Ghost?

---

[10]Dorothy L. Sayers, "The Dogma Is the Drama," in *Creed or Chaos?*, 20.

A: I don't know exactly. He was never seen or heard of till Pentecost. There is a sin against Him which damns you forever, but nobody knows what it is.

Q: What is the doctrine of the Trinity?

A: "The Father incomprehensible, the Son incomprehensible, and the whole thing incomprehensible." Something put in by theologians to make it more difficult—nothing to do with daily life or ethics.[11]

As Sayers reveals with the answer to the question about the Trinity, she worries that, to most people, theology has nothing to do with real life. In "Creed or Chaos?," she responds to this idea by exclaiming, "But if Christian dogma is irrelevant to life, to what, in Heaven's name is it relevant?—since religious dogma is in fact nothing but a statement of doctrines concerning the nature of life and the universe."[12] Throughout her essays, Sayers warns her readers that unless they hold to the truth of doctrine as the keystone of Christianity, the arch of their faith cannot stand.

Sayers, however, recognizes that a lack of doctrinal understanding is not the only threat that Christians must address. She also focuses on the difficulties Christians experience when trying to live out their faith together in community. In an essay discussing the power of evil, Sayers focuses on the ways that evil continually causes division. She declares,

> [Evil] can only work its will by seizing upon some good thing and giving it an ugly and destructive twist, and the good thing which it thus distorts to its own end is that variety and *difference* which ... is found in all created beings. Difference, though it implies

---

[11]Sayers, "The Dogma," 21-22.
[12]Sayers, "Creed or Chaos?," 31.

limitation, is not evil; it only becomes an occasion of evil when a proud and envious will distorts it into division and hatred.[13] Using examples of marital strife and racial prejudice, Sayers shows how easy it is to pervert the differences that should draw us together in community. Rather than recognizing the value of various perspectives and gifts and utilizing them toward a common goal, we all too often use these differences as reasons to isolate ourselves and hate others. To return to the image of the arch, the challenge for communities, then, is not simply the lack of a keystone but also the internal divisions that reveal the stones' flaws that would compromise the arch's stability even with the keystone in place. Throughout her essays, Sayers repeatedly highlights these dangers that she believes threaten to destroy Christianity; but, as we will see, it is in her religious plays that she fully explores the implications of these ideas about doctrine, evil, and community as she presents the various challenges of individuals attempting (and repeatedly failing) to live well in their communities of faith.

Fragmentation and Restoration of Community in *The Zeal Of Thy House* and *The Emperor Constantine*

To explore those challenges, I would like to begin by looking at the ways Sayers crafts the communities in her plays *The Zeal of Thy House* and *The Emperor Constantine*. In these two plays we can see quite clearly how easily evil may pervert good and affect the stability of an entire community. As I mentioned earlier, *The Zeal of Thy House*, which was produced in 1937, is about the rebuilding of Canterbury Cathedral.

---

[13]Dorothy L. Sayers, "Is There a Definite Evil Power That Attacks People in the Same Way as There Is a Good Power That Influences People?," in *Asking Them Questions*, ed. Ronald Selby Wright (New York: Oxford University Press, 1967), 49-50.

Sayers centers the story on William of Sens, the architect, which allows her to explore not only the value of good work as an offering to God but also the danger of pride, for William comes to believe that he is indispensable to the work and must learn to submit his will to God's when he is injured in an accident. William's sin is only part of the problem, however, for Sayers positions him within a religious community where unity is continually threatened by internal divisions.

Sayers highlights these divisions from the beginning, for the audience's first glimpse of the religious community at Canterbury Cathedral comes during a contentious meeting as the brothers struggle to choose an architect for the rebuilding of the cathedral. In the heated debate that ensues, Sayers establishes the differences among them that could easily develop into serious problems. Brother Ernulphus advocates for the stability of an older candidate while Brother Hilary wants a younger, more "progressive" man.[14] Brother Theodatus supports a grand design, repeatedly reminding everyone that since the cathedral is an offering to God, God will provide the money. But Brother Stephen (the treasurer) is afraid of extravagant costs, and Brother Ambrose (the choir master) simply wants good acoustics. None of these differences is necessarily sinful, but they all have the potential to develop into sin because of what they reveal about the brothers' mixed motives and the developing rivalries. As Sayers reveals throughout the rest of the play, the tensions established in this opening scene—and the rivalries that are revealed even more clearly once William is chosen as the architect—repeatedly threaten the peace of this community. Brother Gervase expresses the problem late in the play when he declares, "Jealousy, vanity, hatred, malice and all uncharitableness! And these are churchmen, vowed to holy obedience and humility."[15]

---

[14]ZH, 34-35.
[15]ZH, 103.

Figure 4. The brothers choosing an architect

The most substantial controversy within the community revolves around the question of whether William's lack of virtue in his personal life taints his work on the cathedral, for he is brazenly carrying on an affair with Lady Ursula. While Brother Gervase still admires William's work, declaring that "he thinks of nothing, lives for nothing, but the integrity of his work,"[16] Brother Theodatus asserts that he would rather have a "worse-built church with a more virtuous builder."[17] William is living a sinful life, which, as the Prior warns him, may ultimately have an effect on the work as "the workmen waste their time in gossip and backbiting."[18] But Theodatus is also sinning in his self-righteous condemnation of William, a point that the Prior also calls attention to in his recommendation to Theodatus to "do [his] own work" and "set charity as a bridle on [his] tongue."[19] Rather than coming together to support each other in the great work of rebuilding the cathedral, the brothers are divided and distracted.

---

[16] ZH, 64.
[17] ZH, 79.
[18] ZH, 84.
[19] ZH, 81-82.

Ultimately, Sayers uses William's accident to emphasize the serious consequences of these divisions as they develop into sin. When the sins of each individual come together, they have powerful repercussions not only for William but also for the rest of the community. As William prepares to ascend to the top of the great arch to set the keystone, he asks Theodatus and Simon to carefully check the rope that will help carry him to the top of the arch. William then proceeds to converse with his mistress, whom he has invited to witness his great feat—a conversation that distracts both Theodatus and Simon from their job. The prurient Simon stares at William and Ursula and sings lewd songs as he imagines their relationship, while the "scandalised" Theodatus first averts his eyes from the sinful couple and then closes them as he fervently prays.[20] Neither notices the flaw in the rope that will eventually break under the stress of supporting William. As

Figure 5. Members of the community in *The Zeal of Thy House*

---

[20]*ZH*, 87.

Crystal Downing remarks in her discussion of the play, "The sin is communal."[21] William, Ursula, Simon, and Theodatus all play a part in the disastrous fall from the arch that permanently disables William and threatens to halt progress on the cathedral. Their individual sins come together to damage not only William but also the entire community and its project.

Sayers takes this idea of the communal ramifications of sin even further in *The Emperor Constantine*.[22] In this play, which was produced in 1951 for a festival in the city of Colchester, Sayers traces the life of Constantine and explores the question of whether "Christianity [was] for him a living faith, a profitable superstition, or a cynical instrument of policy."[23] The climax of the play is the Council at Nicaea, and as Sayers explores the disputes that led to the formation of the Nicene Creed, she emphasizes the danger of individual sins that begin to threaten not only the unity of the church but also its witness to the rest of the empire. The issue at stake is, of course, highly important to church doctrine, for the bishops are divided based on their beliefs regarding the relationship between God the Father and God the Son. It is an essential issue and must be settled. But the viciousness of the arguments surrounding the controversy reveals the dangerous instability that characterizes the church even apart from this confusion over doctrine.

Sayers illustrates this problem in a rather humorous scene as people from all over the empire arrive in Nicaea for the council. As a number of people gather in a barbershop, they begin debating the controversy. The theological conversation that ensues is interspersed with angry

---

[21]Crystal Downing, *Writing Performances: The Stages of Dorothy L. Sayers* (New York: Palgrave Macmillan, 2004), 131.
[22]Dorothy L. Sayers, *The Emperor Constantine* (Grand Rapids: Eerdmans, 1976).
[23]Sayers, preface to *The Emperor Constantine*, 6.

complaints, dirty jokes, name-calling, personal insults, and a slanderous accusation against the emperor's mother. It quickly deteriorates into a brawl, and with the stage directions, Sayers emphasizes that the important question of doctrine has been lost: "At this point, the Police, represented by a number of SOLDIERS, arrive on the scene, pushing through the CROWD, which is now shouting impartially for Arius, Alexander, Constantine, and any other names which occur to them—or just shouting."[24] While Sayers makes the most of the humor of this scene, her audience, even while laughing, may remember an earlier scene where Constantine complained about how these divisions in the church were being perceived:

> If you would wait in patience you would set an example of brotherly love to the whole world. But your patience is schism, riot, open denunciation, excommunicated bishops fleeing from one see to another, and proclaiming their wrongs in every Christian pulpit, so that the heathen laugh, and Church and Empire are ashamed.[25]

Not only must the church address this important doctrinal issue to establish a keystone upon which Christians will rely, but it must also address the pervasive sin within the community that makes this dispute so much worse for the church and so destructive to its witness in the rest of the world.

Throughout these two plays, Sayers reminds us that evil does its work "by seizing upon some good thing and giving it an ugly and destructive twist."[26] Productive differences among individuals that could, through honest discussion, lead to better decisions and a clearer conception of

---

[24]*EC*, 129.
[25]*EC*, 110.
[26]Sayers, "A Definite Evil Power?," 49.

truth often lead instead to judgmental anger, self-righteousness, and even violence. In *The Zeal of Thy House*, Sayers develops this idea further by showing how vulnerable everyone is to this perversion of sin—even those who have fully devoted themselves to doing the work that God has given them to do. As I discussed in the first essay, Sayers's goal for any community is good, productive work where individuals by committing themselves to their unique jobs can come together to serve society. But with her portrayal of William of Sens, Sayers illustrates how even this ultimate good for community may be perverted.

Sayers portrays William as being completely committed to "the integrity of his work"[27] even as he leads an immoral life outside of his work, and throughout the play, she emphasizes the important spiritual value of this vocational commitment. She reveals this particularly through the comments of the angels who observe all the actions that take place within the cathedral. When Michael mentions William's immoral life, which is "crammed full of deadly sins,"[28] Gabriel counters this condemnation with remarks on William's work on the cathedral, which is "all well and truly laid without a fault."[29] Raphael agrees with Gabriel, describing William's excellent craftsmanship as a prayer of worship to the "Eternal Architect,"[30] and this perspective is echoed by the Prior, who believes that William's excellence in his craft powerfully reveals "God's glory."[31] As a worker, William seems to fulfill his role perfectly. He is the one who sets the vision for the project and ensures that the community works together effectively to achieve this important task. And it is precisely through his excellent work that Sayers

---

[27] *ZH*, 64.
[28] *ZH*, 53.
[29] *ZH*, 54.
[30] *ZH*, 54.
[31] *ZH*, 79.

illustrates the insidious nature of sin that powerfully corrupts the best motives, changing them into the worst.

William is, in fact, such a good craftsman that he begins to believe that he is not only equal to God but also, in some ways, superior to God, and it is through this sin of pride that Sayers reveals how easily good may be perverted. When speaking with Ursula before he ascends to work on the arch, William declares,

> In making man
> God over-reached Himself and gave away
> His Godhead. He must now depend on man
> For what man's brain, creative and divine
> Can give Him. Man stands equal with Him now,
> Partner and rival. . . .[32]

William then moves from equality to superiority, boasting, "This church is mine / And none but I, not even God, can build it."[33] Rather than placing his masterful work in subjection to God, William arrogantly decides that he is "indispensable."[34] Sayers emphasizes just how dangerous this presumption is, for even as William makes these statements, the archangel Michael is readying his sword to cut the rope when William ascends to the top of the arch. While in the earthly realm William's fall occurs because two of the workers fail to inspect the rope properly, there is also a divine component as Michael enacts the punishment for William's sin of pride. And Sayers's use of symbolism here is quite powerful: William's fall occurs as he attempts to guide the keystone into place in the great arch. By depending upon his own work rather than God's, William has tried to establish himself as

---
[32]*ZH*, 90.
[33]*ZH*, 90.
[34]*ZH*, 90.

the keystone of the arch of this community, and he is punished by God for that presumption.

Sayers does not leave the story there, however, for she offers William a chance to repent. Yet, even with this process of repentance, Sayers continues to illustrate how insidious sin may be in transforming good

Figure 6. William on his sickbed

into evil and perverting the work of community, for William has difficulty even recognizing the sin for which he has been punished. After the accident, William attempts to control the work on the cathedral from his sickbed but finds himself continually hindered by extreme pain. In his frustration, he confesses his sins to the Prior, but even after the Prior absolves him, he still cannot rest. While he has confessed his "lust, greed, wrath, [and] avarice," he has not yet recognized his sin of pride, "the sin that is so much a part of [him]" that he did not realize it was sin.[35] Even when he is confronted by the archangel Michael, William still clings desperately to his pride in his work, declaring,

---

[35]*ZH*, 120.

> I will not yield
> > Nor leave to other men that which is mine,
> > To botch—to alter—turn to something else,
> > Not mine.[36]

William is so wrapped up in the success of his work that he cannot relinquish it to others, even if that is God's will.

William comes to recognize his sin only when Michael reminds him of the example of Jesus, showing him that while Jesus suffered "the bitterest, worst humiliation" at the cross as he "[bowed] His neck under the galling yoke / Frustrate, defeated, half His life unlived, / Nothing achieved," he still had faith that the work of salvation had been accomplished, declaring, "It is finished! . . . when men had thought it scarce begun."[37] Michael also reminds William that Christ, "the Master Architect," left "the work to others," asking them to "feed [His] sheep" while he ascended to heaven.[38] Only then does William acknowledge his sin of pride and agree to let others finish his work, asking that "the Church [will not] / Be lost through [him]."[39] William finally comes to recognize his individual sin and the terrible ramifications it might have on the church community, and he asks that God, in his mercy, not only forgive him but also preserve the community, which has been damaged by his sin.

With these portrayals of sin in *The Zeal of Thy House* and in *The Emperor Constantine*, Sayers emphasizes the intense difficulties involved in preserving communities of faith, for not only is their unity threatened by the conflict that inevitably arises when differences are

---

[36]*ZH*, 123.
[37]*ZH*, 123-24.
[38]*ZH*, 124.
[39]*ZH*, 126.

perverted by sin, but also their ultimate purpose of action may be threatened as individuals begin to serve themselves rather than God. The situations in both plays seem rather bleak. If good is so easily perverted into evil, how can inevitably flawed communities of faith ever come together? In *The Zeal of Thy House* Sayers presents a powerful moment of hope. As the Prior talks about all that William has been able to achieve despite his deep flaws, he declares,

> For God founded His Church, not upon John,
> The loved disciple, that lay so close to His heart
> And knew His mind—not upon John, but Peter;
> Peter the liar, Peter the coward, Peter
> The rock, the common man. John was all gold,
> And gold is rare; the work might wait while God
> Ransacked the corners of the earth to find
> Another John; but Peter is the stone
> Whereof the world is made. . . . [40]

That hope, of God working through the flawed individuals that form his church, is displayed in these two plays. Not only does Sayers state it directly through the Prior's words in *The Zeal of Thy House*, but she also explores it more fully in *The Emperor Constantine* as the church community comes together both to find the truth that will anchor their faith and to care for each other's souls, thereby helping to restore what sin had seemingly destroyed.

In *The Emperor Constantine*, Sayers illustrates that in the midst of all of the dissension, the bishops do eventually manage to work through the challenges of each phrase of the Nicene Creed and arrive at a powerful, clear statement of doctrine, a keystone that anchors the

---

[40] *ZH*, 80.

faith in the truth that we believe in a savior who is "begotten, not made, consubstantial [of one Being] with the Father." And, significantly, this creed is developed through community as the bishops wrestle with the implications of every word. Alexander explains to Constantine how this will work:

> Neither you nor we, Augustus, can dictate to the Holy Ghost.... The decision will not rest with Arius, nor with me—no, nor with the Emperor of the world, but with the lovers of Christ gathered from every land.... Our little wisdoms are not alone, being compassed about with so great a cloud of witnesses, and supported by the prayers of the saints.[41]

With the power of the Holy Spirit and the support of prayer, communities of faith may utilize their differences appropriately to ultimately arrive at truth.

These communities may also come together in powerful acts of love and honesty to help bring individuals to repentance and faith. While the climax of *The Emperor Constantine* is the creation of the Nicene Creed, Sayers's overarching story focuses on Constantine's gradually developing faith. While he quickly sees the political value of allying himself with Christianity and refrains from being baptized until right before his death, Constantine is surrounded by Christians who help guide him to his final decision of faith. As Crystal Downing remarks, "Sayers shows not only the communal writing of dogma . . . but also the communal performance of Constantine's faith."[42] In particular, Sayers illustrates how Constantine's mother, Helena, and his secretary, Togi, provide the love and guidance that he needs at key moments in his life.

---

[41]*EC*, 118-19.
[42]Downing, *Writing Performances*, 132.

Sayers uses these figures most powerfully to help Constantine grapple with the weight of his sin when he murders his son Crispus, mistakenly thinking that Crispus has slept with Constantine's wife. After discovering his mistake, Constantine begins to rave blasphemously to Togi:

> I am lord of the world, like God. I had a son, like God, and like God's Son he was innocent, and I killed him—just like God.... All those solemn old greybeards in Nicaea, wrangling about God's Son, with me sitting there on my golden throne—and none of them knew . . . that I was going to sacrifice my beloved son and be turned into very God![43]

At this point of crisis, Constantine perversely exalts himself in his sin rather than turning to God in repentance, and Sayers uses Togi to remind Constantine not only of the truth of his sin but also of the forgiveness offered by God. Togi first brings Constantine back to reality, declaring, "You're a common sinner like the rest of us, d'you hear?—an ordinary, stupid headstrong man with a violent temper, who has committed a common murder."[44] But then he reminds Constantine where his hope needs to lie, stating, "We are all guilty of Christ's death, and all redeemed by His blood."[45] Togi risks his own life with these blunt remarks, but he does so to help bring Constantine to repentance and salvation. While Constantine, at this point, still cannot completely accept this hope of salvation, he does begin to have a clearer conception of sin, which he later expresses to his mother, declaring, "It is a corruption of life at the source. I and mine are so knit

---

[43]*EC*, 177.
[44]*EC*, 177.
[45]*EC*, 178.

together in evil that no one can tell where the guilt begins or ends."[46] It is at this point that Helena provides the additional support that he needs, for when Constantine cries out, "Mother, tell me, whose blood is on my hands," she echoes Togi's earlier wisdom, declaring, "The blood of God . . . which makes intercession for us,"[47] reminding him again of the truth he has yet to accept. Constantine's conversion is a long process that is not complete until his baptism right before his death, but, as Sayers represents it, Helena and Togi provide the essential guidance he needs to finally accept the truth of Christianity.

With *The Emperor Constantine*, Sayers reveals the hope that, despite their flaws, communities may come together not only to affirm truth but also to help bring others to faith. As she continually demonstrates, however, this hope must ultimately be founded on God and not simply on human work. While sin continually perverts good into evil, God is the one who, as Sayers states in her essay "The Triumph of Easter," "takes our sins and errors and turns them into victories, as He made the crime of the Crucifixion to be the salvation of the world."[48]

Community Through the Atonement in *The Just Vengeance*

Sayers represents this truth most clearly in her play *The Just Vengeance*.[49] In this play, which was produced in 1946 for a festival commemorating the 750th anniversary of Lichfield Cathedral, Sayers crafts the story of an airman who, upon being shot down during the war, is confronted with the realities of what he truly believes. As Sayers describes it, "In that moment, his spirit finds itself drawn into

---

[46]*EC*, 181.
[47]*EC*, 182.
[48]Dorothy L. Sayers, "The Triumph of Easter," in *Creed or Chaos?*, 10.
[49]Dorothy L. Sayers, *The Just Vengeance* (London: Gollancz, 1946).

the fellowship of his native city of Lichfield; there, being shown in an image the meaning of the Atonement, he accepts the Cross, and passes, in that act of choice, from the image to the reality."[50] With this play, Sayers focuses on the power of the atonement both to reconcile humanity to God and to bring individuals into community with each other as they share each other's burdens.

In *The Just Vengeance*, which was heavily influenced by both Dante and Charles Williams, Sayers illustrates the utter brokenness of humanity by emphasizing the truth that without Christ we can never escape the evil of sin, no matter how innocent we would like to see ourselves.[51] Early in the play, the airman distinguishes his own personal creed from the Apostles' Creed that a chorus of people from the city of Lichfield are reciting. Rather than believing "in God, the Father Almighty, Maker of Heaven and earth; and in Jesus Christ," the airman believes

> in man, and in the hope of the future,
> The steady growth of knowledge and power over things,
> The equality of all labouring for the community,
> And a just world where everyone will be happy.[52]

He rejects the idea of "a suffering God" and prefers to place his hope in humanity and the future.[53] Reflecting back on his experiences in the war, however, the airman must acknowledge the truth that achieving a just

---

[50]Sayers, introduction to *JV*, 10.
[51]For a detailed exploration of Dante's influence on Sayers, see Barbara Reynolds's *The Passionate Intellect: Dorothy L. Sayers' Encounter with Dante* (Kent, OH: Kent State University Press, 1989), and for a good explanation of Sayers's interactions with Williams's ideas in her plays, see Suzanne Bray's "Guilt and Glory in Dorothy L. Sayers' and Charles Williams' Festival Plays," *Joint Meeting of the Dorothy L. Sayers Society and the Charles Williams Society October 17, 2007*, ed. Geraldine Perriam (Hurstpierpoint, UK: Dorothy L. Sayers Society, 2010), 13-33.
[52]*JV*, 26.
[53]*JV*, 25.

society is not as easy as his creed suggests, since determining guilt and innocence as a foundation for this just society can prove to be a challenge:

> We try to do right
> > And someone is hurt—very likely the wrong person;
> > And if we do wrong, or even if we do nothing,
> > It comes to the same in the end. We drop a bomb
> > And condemn a thousand people to sudden death,
> > The guiltless along with the guilty. Or we refuse
> > To drop a bomb, and condemn a thousand people
> > To a lingering death in a concentration camp
> > As surely as if we had set our hands to the warrant.[54]

While the airman recognizes this challenge, he initially refuses to accept his own complicity in the shared guilt of sin that makes his dream of perfect human justice impossible. He instead attempts to escape the guilt he feels over his actions in the war by blaming others, crying, "It was not my fault, but the fault of the old people."[55] At that point, however, the chorus takes up his cry and echoes it with "generation after generation" blaming the ones that came before, compelling the airman to eventually realize that he, too, will be judged and found guilty by the next generation.[56] He finally acknowledges his own complicity, declaring to the chorus, "Forgive me. I was wrong: we are victims together / Or guilty together."[57]

With this opening to the play, Sayers reveals why the airman's vision of justice will never be achieved as he begins to realize the impossibility of humans ever establishing a foundation of true innocence from

---

[54] *JV*, 17-18.
[55] *JV*, 27.
[56] *JV*, 27.
[57] *JV*, 28.

which to enact it. As Sayers reflects in the introduction to her translation of Dante's *Purgatorio*, "We are all too much involved in the common guilt—part wrongers and partly wronged—ever to be sure of a perfectly pure motive for what we do."[58] The airman begins to grasp this truth at the beginning of the play, and as the play continues, Sayers takes him through the process of recognizing that the suffering God, whom he initially rejected, is the airman's only hope for true justice.

Significantly, Sayers has this process occur within the context of community. As the Recording Angel of the city tells him, the airman has been drawn back to his home in this moment of death because it is for him a "god-bearing image" that has the potential to draw him to the truth of Christ.[59] This idea, which Sayers borrows from Dante and Williams, is the core of the play, for the airman must allow his love for his city to draw him back not only into its community but, more importantly, into the community of the church. Initially, when the airman tries to distance himself from the city by affirming his own creed in opposition to the Apostles' Creed, which he inadvertently finds himself reciting, the Recording Angel tells him:

> What is speaking in you is the voice of the city,
> The Church and the household of Christ, your people
>   and country
> From where you derive. Did you think you were unbegotten?
> Unfranchised? With no community and no past?
>   Out of the darkness of your unconscious memory
>   The stones of the city are crying out. . . .[60]

---

[58] Dorothy L. Sayers, introduction to *The Divine Comedy 2: Purgatory* by Dante Alighieri, trans. Dorothy L. Sayers (New York: Penguin, 1955), 57.
[59] *JV*, 23.
[60] *JV*, 24.

As the airman comes to identify himself with this community, he begins to understand even more deeply both the utter brokenness of humanity and the perfect sacrifice of Christ that provides our only hope.

Sayers emphasizes this point by having the members of the city act out moments from Scripture to help the airman "fully understand" the truth of humanity's guilt and Christ's atonement.[61] The airman is drawn into this play-within-a-play as the Recording Angel introduces him to Eve. Initially, he begins to pose his questions about good, evil, and justice directly to her. Eventually, however, he becomes simply an observer as the city begins to answer his questions by presenting the tragedy of Cain and Abel and emphasizing the truth that "all / Suffer with Abel and destroy with Cain, / Each one at once the victim and the avenger."[62] With this retelling, the city reminds the airman that the innocence he tries to claim for himself is impossible for anyone to achieve because all are tainted even in their seeming innocence. Once this truth has resonated within the airman's thoughts, the community then illustrates for him the "just vengeance" of Christ's perfect sacrifice as the same chorus members who presented the story of Cain and Abel act out Jesus' birth, trial, and crucifixion, revealing that

> Only the soul that has never consented to sin
> And is not concerned to justify itself
> Can accept the whole guilt—the open injustice
> And the hidden iniquity in the heart of equity—
> Carry them away, purge them and sterilise them
> Taking them into itself and making conclusion.[63]

And it is here that the airman is drawn fully not only into the community of the city of Lichfield but also into the community of the

---

[61] *JV*, 29.
[62] *JV*, 43.
[63] *JV*, 69.

church as he himself participates in the reenactment. At first, he remains in the role of the questioner, striving to understand both God's law and Christ's sacrifice by questioning Jesus directly during his trial before Caiaphas. But then the airman surprises himself as he cries, "Crucify! Crucify!" along with the crowd,[64] becoming complicit in the sin that he has been trying to escape. Finally, he comes to recognize the truth that only Christ, as both God and man, can provide the perfect sacrifice to atone for humanity, and he decides to enter that truth by helping to carry the cross. At the climax of the play, when Jesus begins to carry his cross on the way to the crucifixion, the Recording Angel asks, "Who will carry the cross and share the burden of God . . . ?"[65] The members of the chorus and the airman himself all rush to help, creating a powerful image as these individuals come together as the church both to accept the work of the atonement and to respond to it by bearing Jesus' cross as well as each other's burdens.

Interestingly, when the play was first presented at Lichfield Cathedral, the dean of the cathedral questioned the staging of this scene, worrying that the sight of the people helping Jesus carry his cross up and down the aisles of the cathedral might not be reverent enough. Sayers responded forcefully, declaring, "The carrying of the Cross by the Faithful is the point of the play—it *is* the play."[66] For Sayers, this moment of the play powerfully illustrates the two components she believes are essential to our understanding of the atonement: the act reconciles individuals to God *and* unites all of us to each other. By taking up the cross, the members of this community are physically enacting their choice to follow Christ and accept his sacrifice for their sins,

---

[64]*JV*, 66.
[65]*JV*, 72.
[66]Dorothy L. Sayers, *The Letters of Dorothy L. Sayers 1944 to 1950: A Noble Daring*, vol. 3, ed. Barbara Reynolds (Cambridge: Dorothy L. Sayers Society, 1998), 191.

and they are also demonstrating their willingness to carry the burdens of others in their community. As the various individuals run to take up the cross, they each declare a different burden that they are willing to carry, such as "shame," "toil," "pain," or "bitterness"[67]—burdens that correlate directly to ways they have been injured by others.

With her focus on the ways that the atonement allows for individual Christians to share the burdens of others, Sayers draws on Charles Williams's ideas to attempt to explain how the atonement might affect the realities of daily life. In a letter to James Welch in November of 1943 Sayers asks, "Why does *crucified God* make more difference to washing-day than Socrates drinking hemlock? If it doesn't, why call yourselves Christians?"[68] She then proceeds to answer the question with a very practical example of how the atonement might work in daily life as we bear the sin of others. She remarks,

> When we have to do without a fire on a cold night to save fuel, we (comparatively innocent) are to that extent "carrying" the stupidity of the ministers (political ministers, I mean, not parsons!), the tiresomeness and lack of charity between miners and owners, and the guilt of war which makes extra coal necessary. By our willing acceptance of that "little daily crucifixion" the deficity is wiped out and the evil sterilised. It finishes there. . . . We *take* the other people's guilt and carry it, and so atone for it and there's an end. If we refuse, then the evil continues to propagate itself—armies are destroyed and battles lost for lack of coal. Or if we violently resent the sacrifice, we start a fresh cycle of anger and hatred and trouble.[69]

---

[67]JV, 72.
[68]Dorothy L. Sayers, *Letter to James Welch, November 11, 1943* (Dorothy L. Sayers Papers, Folder 434a, the Marion E. Wade Center, Wheaton College, Wheaton, IL).
[69]Sayers, *Letter to James Welch*.

As Suzanne Bray describes it, "For Sayers, this carrying of the guilt by Christ is the way he 'makes evil good in and through the working of the Law of Sin.' It is also . . . the prototype of the way that Christians, as part of Christ's body, can play their part in the work of transforming evil into good on a daily basis through acts which both follow and complement the forgiveness of sins."[70] For Sayers, this vision of the atonement provides, first, the keystone of Christ's perfect sacrifice that stabilizes the arch of the church and, second, a model for the way individual Christians may actually bear the burdens of others as they fulfill their roles as stones within that arch. While, as we have seen, these ideas are embedded throughout the three plays discussed in this essay, Sayers reveals them most completely in *The Just Vengeance* through this powerful moment where the airman joins all the other flawed and broken members of the church as they run to help carry the cross.

Theater as a Model of True Community

Sayers discusses these ideas about Christian community in many of her essays and letters, but it is truly in *The Just Vengeance*, *The Emperor Constantine*, and *The Zeal of Thy House* that she reveals the complexities involved and provides the powerful images that help her audiences understand them. And I believe it is significant that Sayers expresses these ideas most fully through drama. As she began to learn more about the craft of theater and the ways that theater professionals come together to produce a play, she began to see theater as a much better example of a successful community of faith than the contemporary church.

When Sayers began writing for the theater, she knew that she had much to learn. While she had the enthusiasm of an amateur, stemming

---

[70]Bray, "Guilt and Glory," 18.

from her childhood love of theatricals, she did not have any professional experience. She therefore relied heavily on other professionals to effectively integrate her into their community. Her first play, *Busman's Honeymoon*, was a collaboration with her friend Muriel St. Clare Byrne, who taught at the Royal Academy of Dramatic Art. With *The Zeal of Thy House*, she turned for help to her experienced production team: Harcourt Williams (a well-known actor who had been the artistic director of the Old Vic Theatre in London), Frank Napier (an actor and director at the Old Vic), Elizabeth Haffenden (a costume designer who would later win Academy Awards for her designs for *Ben Hur* and *A Man for All Seasons*), and Laurence Irving (a set designer who had been working in Hollywood). Her letters to them are full of requests for help as she seeks to master this new medium, and she is, perhaps surprisingly, remarkably humble regarding her place within this new community.

Generally, when Sayers discusses the craft of writing, she presents herself as the ultimate expert: she knows her job and does it well, and woe to anyone who questions that. As a playwright, however, Sayers is generally humble and generous. She recognizes that she plays only a part in the success of the final production, and she is willing to take the advice of experts even when it comes to how she crafts the play. In a letter to Irving, for instance, she defers to his opinion, remarking, "Having as a dramatist, become enamoured of my own work, I am inclined to urge the cutting down of the pageant rather than of the four Acts of the play proper; but you will use your own judgement about this."[71] In addition, Sayers resists the inclination to dictate every element of a production with copious stage directions. She

---

[71]Dorothy L. Sayers, *The Letters of Dorothy L. Sayers 1937 to 1943: From Novelist to Playwright*, vol. 2, ed. Barbara Reynolds (New York: St. Martin's, 1997), 14.

leaves it to the experts to interpret the play effectively from the foundation that she has laid for them. When writing *The Just Vengeance*, for instance, Sayers describes her play as "a working playwright's script, containing nothing but straightforward directions to a producer who will know how to interpret them," and she warns that "if the playwright tries to prescribe every movement and every tone of voice he merely gets in the way of the actors and hampers the production."[72] In a poem to Harcourt Williams, she even describes her play as "dull, deaf senseless ink and paper" until it receives life through an actual production.[73]

As a novelist, Sayers describes the powerful ways individuals could come together in community and use their skills to help transform society, but as a playwright, she experiences that kind of power for herself. She recognizes that everyone in the production must first be unified with a common truth (the success of the play) and then must be committed not only to doing their own individual work with excellence but also to supporting the expertise of the rest of the community. Only with that kind of focus, passion, and humility would the final goal be achieved.

The powerful significance of this for Sayers is revealed in a talk that she delivers at the Malvern Conference in 1941, where she was invited to speak on the church's witness in society. When thinking about the powerful "unifying bond" that should exist among Christians, she asks a series of questions:

> Do I . . . immediately feel at home with Christians of any class or nationality—*more* at home with them than with non-Christians

---

[72]Sayers, *Letters*, 3:193.
[73]Dorothy L. Sayers, "To the Interpreter Harcourt Williams," in *Two Plays About God and Man: The Devil to Pay, He That Should Come* (New York: Vineyard, 1977), 9.

of my own nation and class? Should I in a casual encounter of a few hours . . . find the Christians unhesitatingly discovering one another and plunged into animated discussion of their common interests and experiences? Am I sure that they are organized by a discipline which, overriding all conflicting considerations will, when a crisis occurs, make them toe the line as one man? Do I feel that, tiresome, stupid, selfish, quarrelsome, pig-headed and infuriating as they may individually be, I would rather be associated with them in the most laborious and painful devotion to our common ends, than with any other set of people on earth in any other pursuit imaginable?[74]

Sayers then confesses that she must answer no to these questions, and she is struck by the fact that she has found that kind of community not in the church but in the theater.[75] She declares,

I know that, if their stomachs are aching, their parents dying, their wives deserting them and the whole company quarrelling like cats, a rigid discipline will find them at their posts when the curtain rises; that they are conscious, even if dumbly and vaguely, of a tremendous traditional solidarity, reaching so far back into the past as to make the Christian Church look like a mushroom of a night's growth. . . . Above all, I am conscious of that rooted loyalty to something outside themselves which is expressed in the threadbare formula, "the show must go on"; and which not only makes toil and fatigue and hardship and difficulty negligible, but transforms them into a kind of arduous pleasure. And

---

[74]Dorothy L. Sayers, "The Church's Responsibility," in *Malvern, 1941: The Life of the Church and the Order of Society. Being the Proceedings of the Archbishop of York's Conference* (London: Longman's Green, 1941), 58.
[75]Sayers, "Church's Responsibility," 58.

because of these things, I recognize in the theatre all the stigmata of a real and living Church.[76]

Theater, for Sayers, has all the qualities that she desired to see in the church, so it seems fitting that she uses drama to explore the challenges facing communities of faith. With these plays, Sayers not only reflects on the qualities that communities of faith need in order to thrive, but she also enacts these qualities within each of the communities that came together in making the productions.

Sayers may have experienced her ideal community of faith much more fully in the theater than in the church, but she never abandoned the idea that the church could become a more effective community of faith. While she repeatedly reveals in her plays just how difficult it is for common, flawed stones to come together and form a perfect arch, she also demonstrates that by looking to Christ as the keystone that holds us together and by sharing the burden with others as we work together to support that truth, we may help preserve the arch of the Christian community and serve God effectively. In addition, Sayers recognizes the powerfully transformative work of Christ through the atonement. While acknowledging that we may only be common flawed stones like

Figure 7. Sayers at rehearsal

---

[76]Sayers, "Church's Responsibility," 59-60.

Peter, she trusts that Christ, "being the alchemist's stone . . . [can] turn stone to gold, and purge the gold itself / From dross, till all is gold."[77] This is Sayers's ultimate vision for communities of faith.

---

[77] *ZH*, 80-81.

RESPONSE

Andy Mangin

In 1984, Wheaton College's Arena Theater got a new space. Jenks Hall had been purchased that spring and the theater was moving from the basement of Fischer dorm. The basement of Fischer dorm was quite a place to do theater. Space was limited, with low ceilings and the audience stacked on walls. As the story goes, they used to bribe the dorm floor above the theater with pizza during shows to keep the residents from flushing the toilet. Nothing quite ruins a tender moment of theater like the sound of dorm plumbing. Jim Young, the director of the theater at that time, had been praying fervently for a new space and was excited to move in. Jim and the theater students carried all the set pieces, furniture, clothing racks, and props across campus in what must have been a wild procession. Once everything had been moved out of Fischer and there was no object left to carry, they began the process of carrying something else. Jim believed the prayers of all those who had worked in that basement were in the walls. So the students put their hands against the walls in Fischer, and in the last leg of the procession, the students carried those prayers to the new space in Jenks and placed them into the walls. They literally carried the prayers from one building to the other. This is a powerful image of both prayer and community. It's a perfect story of how theater had given Jim and those students a way to embody belief and give it action. And it served to connect them to a community of the past, present, and future.

In Arena Theater, this tradition is still in practice today. Each school year we start with a time of prayer during which we put our hands on the walls of the theater. And we add to the prayers. I have learned, through the practice of theater, that things matter, prayer matters, and embodiment matters. Jim Young loved the work of Dorothy Sayers. He taught her plays every year. He directed *The Zeal of Thy House* in 1978 at Wheaton College. And I believe Dorothy Sayers would have loved Jim Young and that story of carried prayers. It is that very kind of display of belief, community, and action that Sayers recognized in her address at the Malvern Conference in 1941: "I recognize in the theater all the stigmata of the Real and Living Church."[1]

As Dr. Colón has clearly laid out for us, there was something important and transformative for Sayers in the theater. Dorothy Sayers was intrigued and engaged by the community of theater makers united in the goal of putting on a play. I want to go further and explore the levels of community possible in the theater, not only in the process of theater making but also in the audience's experience of that creation. Theater is the only art form in which both the medium and the subject are human. It seeks to explore who we are; it is a laboratory of the human condition. In order to do this work well and with honesty, theater is dependent on a series of collaborations, each requiring belief, commitment, and relationship. This call to community and away from isolation is the very thing Colón is pointing us toward in Dorothy Sayers's work.

A play, unlike other written material, is unfinished until this collaboration begins. "That is why all good stage scripts read rather

---

[1] Dorothy L. Sayers, "The Church's Responsibility," in *Malvern, 1941: The Life of the Church and the Order of Society. Being the Proceedings of the Archbishop of York's Conference* (London: Longman's Green, 1941), 58.

crudely and badly," Sayers wrote in a letter. "If the playwright tries to prescribe every movement or tone of voice he merely gets in the way of the actors and hampers the production."[2] Sayers, who had primarily written novels, would be working in a different way with the material for her plays. But she was energized by this collaborative model, perhaps out of that hunger for community she had sought in other arenas. In 1936, beginning with *The Zeal of Thy House,* she entered the theater world in a way that was new for her and saw how theater was made from the inside. In the early days of the production of a play, a group of designers and a director will sit down and bring their visual experience and storytelling acumen to the material. Each is intensely focused on their own phase of the production—set, costumes, lights, music, and so on—but all in the shared service of the script. They must complement one other to allow the story to be clear.

When I'm directing a play, I find this collaborative process to be enormously helpful. It is in these first few meetings that the play begins to become clear. These initial meetings give life to the script, which is essentially dead material, and are the very important first step in the collaborative process. The play is drawn out of the study in which it was written and into a world where others begin to engage with it artistically. Designers and directors wrestle with the play to try to tell its story to the audience, lifting it quite literally from the script to the stage. Then a play goes into rehearsal, where it gains another important set of collaborators, the actors.

Here is an excerpt from Dorothy Sayers's poem *To the Interpreter Harcourt Williams:*

---

[2]Dorothy L. Sayers, *The Letters of Dorothy L. Sayers 1944 to 1950, Vol. 3,* ed. Barbara Reynolds (Cambridge: Dorothy L. Sayers Society, 1999), 193.

So is the play, save by the actor's making,
No play, but dull, deaf senseless ink and paper,
Either for either made: Light, eye; sense, spirit;
Ear, sound; gift, gold; play, actor; speech and knowing,
Become themselves by what themselves inherit
From their sole heirs, receiving and bestowing;
Thus, then, do thou, taking what thou dost give,
Live in these lines, by whom alone they live.[3]

Sayers describes beautifully the embodiment that is necessary in the process of a character coming to life. She admires Harcourt Williams, an actor who played multiple roles in her plays, including William of Sens in that original production of *The Zeal of Thy House*. She recognizes that without the actor, the lines are dead, and by extension, so are the characters.

I'm reminded of another Jim Young story. In one of his classes, two actors were working on a Shakespeare scene. Although they had memorized their lines, they hadn't rehearsed as much as they should have to present the scene in class. According to one of the actors, they believed they could stumble their way through it. Because they felt awkward that they were not ready, they did not take it seriously, even laughing at themselves at times. When they finished the scene, Jim Young put down his clipboard and left the room. The actors and the rest of the class didn't know what to do. When he came back a few minutes later, it was clear he had been crying. According to those who were there, he said something like, "These characters are real. They are stuck on a page and you are their only chance to have life. An audience will never know them if you do that to them. They will never live. That

---

[3]Dorothy L. Sayers, *Four Sacred Plays* (Deerfield Beach: Oxford City Press, 2011), 107.

is your responsibility and this is what you do? How would you like it if someone told your story like that?"

Apparently, there wasn't a dry eye in the class. It's a lot to demand of a college student, but that was Jim. He was moved by the process of the characters coming to life. It is an almost holy act of transformation, the deepest kind of empathy. Such empathy is possible through the practice of embodiment, through extended imagination, and through a commitment to love the character. In justifying and advocating for a character, an actor will often discover how similar they are to a character. I have always found sound theatrical reasoning and practice in the phrase *There but for the grace of God, go I.*

It is out of this internal collaboration—actor with character—that the play begins to come to life more deeply. The human beings come out of it embodied and relatable. But theater is dependent on yet another, and perhaps most important, phase of collaboration. Unlike film, theater is dependent on a live audience. This is not to say that there is not a vital process that happens in the rehearsal hall. But every rehearsal, every set and costume, and all the intense focus in preparation are pointed toward the future audience. Theater is dependent on an audience—and not a passive one. In the theater, the audience is being asked to be more than consumers. They are being asked to engage and participate. They are being asked to be co-creators of the play. Dorothy Sayers knew that the audience was necessary for a play to work. In the words of the Recorder at the very beginning of *A Just Vengeance*,

> Playing all the parts as best we may. But yet
> We, who are actors, bid you not forget
> That all these images on which you look
> Are but pictures painted in a book—
> No more like they that bid you think upon

> Than this yellow disc is like the sun;
> Though, in a picture, this might stand for that,
> And the great sun take no offence thereat.[4]

This is similar to William Shakespeare's prologue in *Henry V*:

> Piece out our imperfections with your thoughts;
> Into a thousand parts divide one man,
> And make imaginary puissance;
> Think when we talk of horses, that you see them
> Printing their proud hoofs i' the receiving earth;
> For 'tis your thoughts that now must deck our kings.[5]

It is a challenge and a call to recognize that there will be holes and that the audience will need to step into the gap. As the great theater director Peter Brook wrote in *The Empty Space*, "The only thing that all forms of theater have in common is the need for an audience. This is more than a truism: in the theatre the audience completes the steps of creation."[6] The audience is necessary for theater to work.

Ayad Akhtar, the playwright, described the experience this way in a recent essay in *The New York Times*:

> A living being before a living audience. Relationship unmediated by the contemporary disembodying screen. Not the appearance of a person, but the reality of one. Not a simulacrum of a relationship, but a form of actual relationship. The situation of all theater, a situation that can awaken in us a recollection of something more primordial, religious ritual... the act of gathering to

---

[4]Sayers, *Four Sacred Plays*, 281.
[5]William Shakespeare, *King Henry V* (London: Routledge, 1988), 7.
[6]Peter Brook, *The Empty Space* (New York: Touchstone, 1968), 127.

witness the myths of our alleged origins enacted—this is the root of the theater's timeless magic.[7]

This connection in the moment between performer and audience, this shared experience of a glimpse of humanity, demands something of us. It asks us to tell the story too. An audience, inclining and co-creating, might be able to experience things they might never experience in their own lives. It gives us a chance to see the embodied stories about the extremes of humanity, times we might never face; yet in it, we might also recognize ourselves. And importantly, out of this last collaboration can come reflection. The great paradox of theater is this: an audience is being asked to look past themselves, to engage in a story about others with the hope that who they are will be reflected back at them.

Arthur Miller wrote about the role of the audience while watching a play:

> My conception of the audience is of a public each member of which is carrying about with him what he thinks is an anxiety, or a hope, or a preoccupation which is his alone and isolates him from mankind; and in this respect at least the function of a play is to reveal him to himself so that he may touch others by virtue of the revelation of his mutuality with them. If only for this reason I regard the theater as a serious business, one that makes or should make man more human, which is to say, less alone.[8]

In this way, the theater fights isolation. It allows us to see that our struggles with life and sin are not unique. Theater can allow us to see

---

[7]Ayad Akhtar, "One Mind, One Heart, One Body," *New York Times* 30 (Dec 2017): AR 5.
[8]Arthur Miller, *Arthur Miller's Collected Plays: With an Introduction* (New York: Viking Press, 1957), 11.

how interconnected we really are. *There but for the grace of God, go I.* How can we fit into the arch Colón has described until we see how we are similar? I have had this experience of connectivity many times as an audience member, and I know of many other stories of people who were shown something like this by a play. This kind of experience often sneaks up on you. It is often revealed where and how you least expect it. And even that reflection doesn't happen in isolation; it happens while you are sitting in a crowd. The theater is not for single viewing. It is not for private consumption. It does not take place on your phone. You are meant to be sitting with others, laughing when they laugh, crying when they cry—in some cases, moved to do so by those around you. This is what the ancient Greeks would call *catharsis*. Catharsis is a release of those emotions caused by viewing or experiencing art. It was believed that out of catharsis could come restoration and renewal. It could cause realization and change.

    I had the unique opportunity to be involved in a play based on the poems of my late colleague and friend Brett Foster. Brett had been fighting cancer for some time, and an idea developed to dramatize and embody his poems in a night of theater. The title was taken from one of his poems, "The Future Belongs to the Good Old Days." We rehearsed for several months, collaborating with Brett on which poems might work. He gave us new material that he was still working on. At that point, we didn't know what it would be or how it would work. But we started the work, connecting to the truths of life and death in his poetry. There was so much humanity in his work as he struggled with the sickness. There were poems about doctors and airports and his family. As we worked toward an opening night, our friend became more ill. During our first performance, Brett went to be with the Lord. The audience that night was made up of people who knew Brett and who wanted to celebrate his work. We were also celebrating his life as we communed in the theater that night. I will never forget the faces of his friends in the audience. I, an actor, and they, the audience, were sharing a moment that could never be repeated. Rarely is the moment as charged as this. And yet, this very thing is the power of theater. The shared experience, live and ephemeral, affected and changed by a live audience, is a recipe for community.

Dorothy Sayers clearly loved the theater. She deeply connected to the artists who worked on her plays and found in them, as Colón has shown us, a community that she saw as unique—even in comparison to the church. On a deeper level, her plays were asking questions about what it means to be a human, what it means to be redeemed. And she was able to do it because designers brought her plays off the page, actors brought their characters to life, and audiences connected to what they saw. Unlike her novels, her characters could come to life on the stage. Plays are embodied by real, living human beings, being watched by other human beings, who could watch the characters actually breathe, fight, and change. And in this way, she could draw a community into questions about who they were and how they could fit into "the arch." She could ask them what their keystone would be. And as Colón has shown us, she hoped to draw them toward each other, toward reflection, and toward action.

3

DOROTHY L. SAYERS'S VISION FOR COMMUNITIES OF JOY

TO BEGIN THIS ESSAY, I WOULD LIKE to reflect on the two images that I have used to illustrate Sayers's ideas about communities of action and communities of faith: the complexities of change ringing that she explores in *The Nine Tailors* and the challenges of constructing an arch that appear in *The Zeal of Thy House*. As we consider these images, we get a sense of the intense work that Sayers believes is necessary to maintain strong Christian community. Change ringing, which requires both the physical stamina to pull a heavy church bell and the mental stamina to keep track of the intricate patterns that make up each peal, is a complex art. These complexities are what make it an apt image for Sayers's ideas regarding communities of action as she envisions individuals finding their particular vocations and then working diligently in harmony with others to help transform the world. Building an arch is perhaps even more complex than change ringing as builders work carefully to balance the "interlocking stresses"[1] of the stones so that they may be anchored together by a

---

[1] Dorothy L. Sayers, *The Zeal of Thy House* (Eugene, OR: Wipf & Stock, 2011), 59.

perfectly placed keystone. As Sayers demonstrates in her religious plays, the precise balance of Christian community, which requires both upholding the centering truth of doctrine and supporting the other members, is always in danger of toppling without constant care and attention. Individually, each image illustrates how challenging Sayers believes it is to maintain strong communities, and when we consider both together, the work involved seems almost impossible or, at the very least, exhausting.

Sayers herself was no stranger to hard work. She would regularly juggle multiple projects, and she always fully committed herself to doing whatever was necessary to complete those projects successfully. For *The Nine Tailors*, for instance, she immersed herself in the intricacies of change ringing so that she could get the details right for her mystery; and for her plays, she even went so far as to help construct costumes and props. Sayers's life, however, was not one of drudgery where she diligently—but perhaps a little resentfully—did her duty. Sayers's life was characterized by joy, and it was a type of joy that often overflowed into silliness and fun. As Norah Lambourne, the costume designer for several of Sayers's plays, recounts, "[Sayers's] presence was always welcome in the work room, especially at times of crisis or near-panic when she could always say the right thing to make everyone laugh and relax!"[2] For Sayers, joy is just as vital a component for good, strong community as hard work and true faith, which is why for this final essay, I would like to focus on this quality of joy. I will first explore how joy manifested itself in Sayers's own life as she interacted with various communities; then, second, I will turn to her detective novels to see how Sayers illustrates this important connection between joy and community through the way she develops the character of Harriet Vane.

---

[2]Norah Lambourne, "Dorothy L. Sayers: Her Little-Known Manual Skills," in *Studies in Sayers*, ed. Christopher Dean (Hurstpierpoint, UK: Dorothy L. Sayers Society, 1994), 5.

Sayers and the Joy of Friendship

In an essay titled "'Generosity and Courtesy': Dorothy L. Sayers as Friend," Marjorie Lamp Mead references an early poem by Sayers entitled "Hymn in Contemplation of Sudden Death." In this poem, Sayers thanks God for the various blessings in her life. She begins with her friends:

> LORD, if this night my journey end
> I thank Thee first for many a friend,
> The sturdy and unquestioned piers
> That run beneath my bridge of years.[3]

As Mead states in her essay, "Friends were not a luxury in Sayers' life, enjoyed but not essential; rather friends were foundational, as necessary to Sayers as the very air she breathed."[4] Sayers loved being in community, and she devoted a significant amount of time to developing and maintaining strong friendships, particularly through her letters, which are full of a sense of joy. Not only would Sayers cheerfully engage her friends and family with in-depth discussions of their mutual interests, but she might also include a silly story or a fanciful illustration designed solely to make the recipient of her letter laugh: a sketch of a relative being dragged off to the insane asylum after being asked too many questions from Sayers's young son, or a series of drawings showing where her cat's latest progeny had ended up. As Norah Lambourne remarked, "Dorothy was a superb letter writer. One always opened one of her letters in joyful anticipation of the contents."[5]

---

[3]Dorothy L. Sayers, "Hymn in Contemplation of Sudden Death," in *Poetry of Dorothy L. Sayers*, ed. Ralph E. Hone (Trowbridge, UK: The Dorothy L. Sayers Society, 1996), 78.

[4]Marjorie Lamp Mead, "'Generosity and Courtesy': Dorothy L. Sayers as Friend," in *Studies in Sayers*, ed. Christopher Dean (Hurstpierpoint, UK: The Dorothy L. Sayers Society, 1994), 8.

[5]Lambourne, "Dorothy L. Sayers," 6.

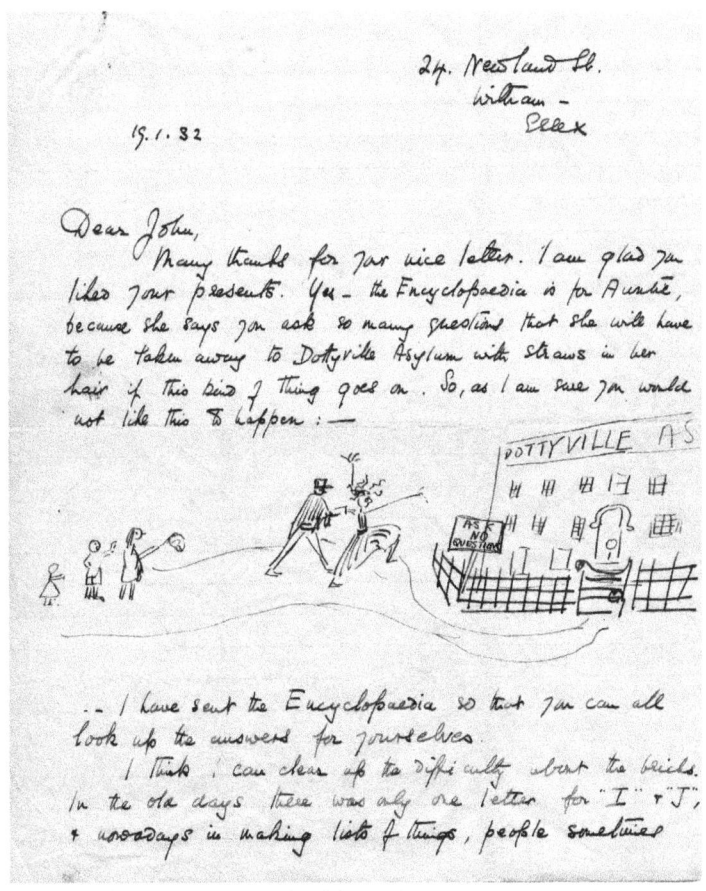

Figure 8. Aunt Ivy going to the asylum

Sayers's correspondence with C. S. Lewis is characteristic of the way that she developed and maintained friendships through her joyful letters. Many of their letters address serious topics such as Sayers's translation of Dante, or a volume of essays that was being published as a tribute to their mutual friend Charles Williams, or even Lewis's grief over his wife's illness. But much of the correspondence is silly and humorous, such as a sketch of a dog standing outside a closed door

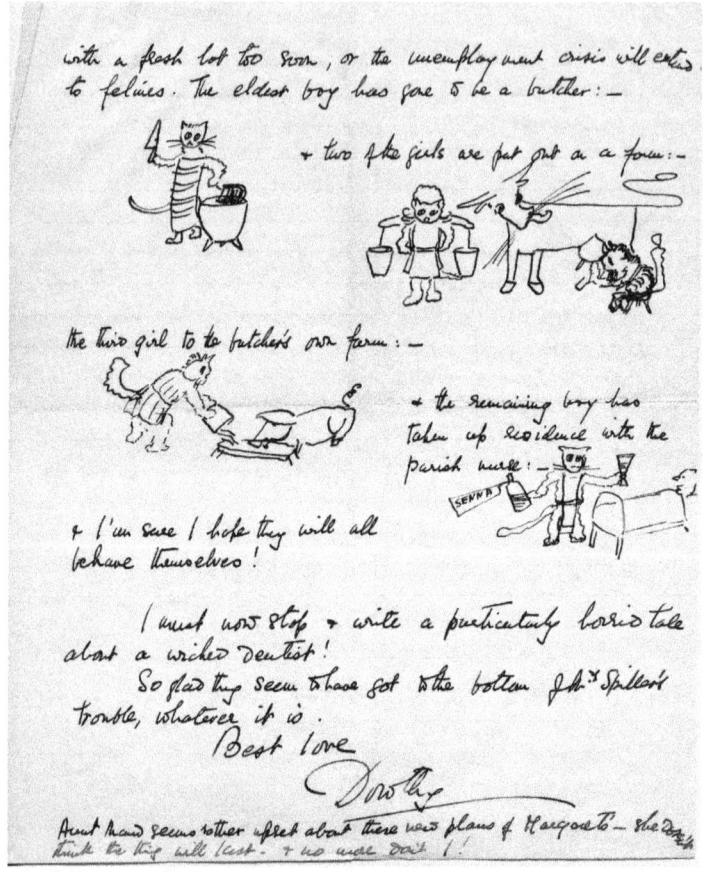

Figure 9. Sayers's kittens working on their new homes

complete with an "UNWELCOME" mat and a "WORKING—KEEP OUT" sign that Sayers included in a letter where she complains about being pestered to death by a correspondent.[6] Or there is Sayers's response to Lewis when she discovers that his stepsons have pet mice

---

[6]Dorothy L. Sayers, *Letter to C. S. Lewis, May 13, 1943* (Dorothy L. Sayers Papers, Folder 96, The Marion E. Wade Center, Wheaton College, Wheaton, IL).

and are therefore not interested in receiving one of her kittens. She complains, "The domestic factory goes on churning out Kittens. . . . But there! What's the good of talking? Obviously I cannot work any Kittens off on *you*. Never mind; we all have our troubles."[7] My favorite exchange, though, is one in which Sayers tells Lewis about her newly-acquired chickens, which she has decided to name after characters in a novel by Jane Austen:

> I have no news, except that—looking forward to the confidently-expected food-crisis, I have purchased two Hens. In their habits they display, respectively Sense and Sensibility, and I have therefore named them Elinor and Marianne. Elinor is a round, comfortable, motherly-looking little body, who lays one steady, regular, undistinguished egg per day, and allows nothing to disturb her equanimity. . . . Marianne is leggier, timid, and liable to hysterics. Sometime she lays a shell-less egg, sometimes a double yolk, sometimes no egg at all. On the days when she lays no egg she nevertheless goes and sits in the nest for the usual time, and seems to imagine that nothing more is required. As my gardener says: "She just *thinks* she's laid an egg." Too much imagination—in fact, Sensibility. But when she does lay an egg it is larger than Elinor's. But you cannot wish to listen to this cackle.[8]

Lewis did, however, "wish to listen to this cackle," for he responds, "I loved hearing about Elinor and Marianne. You are a real letter writer."[9]

---

[7]Dorothy L. Sayers, *Letter to C. S. Lewis, July 3, 1957* (Dorothy L. Sayers Papers, Folder 94, The Marion E. Wade Center, Wheaton College, Wheaton, IL).
[8]Dorothy L. Sayers, *The Letters of Dorothy L. Sayers 1944 to 1950: A Noble Daring*, vol. 3, ed. Barbara Reynolds (Cambridge: Dorothy L. Sayers Society, 1999), 305.
[9]C. S. Lewis, "Letter to Dorothy L. Sayers, June 5, 1947," in *The Collected Letters of C. S. Lewis, Volume II: Books, Broadcasts, and the War, 1931–1949*, ed. Walter Hooper (New York: Harper Collins, 2004), 779.

Sayers's correspondence with Lewis, as well as with many of her other friends, reveals the joy that she experienced in her friendships, a joy that was, in fact, an integral part of her personality. Significantly, as Sayers continues her "Hymn in Contemplation of Sudden Death," she thanks God not only for her friends but also

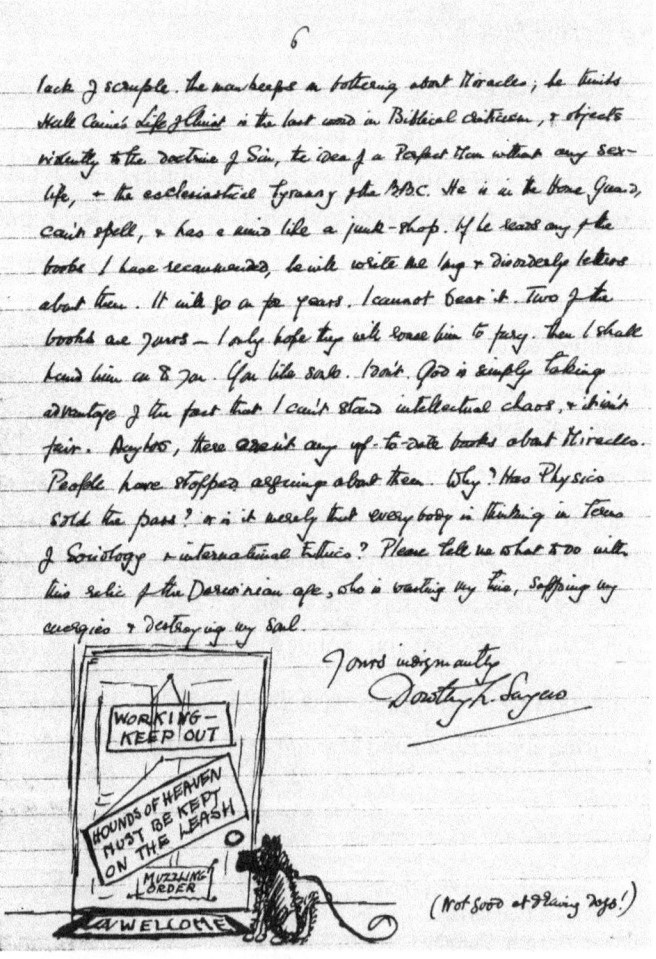

Figure 10. Sayers's protection from persistent correspondents

For the power thou gavest me
 To view the whole world mirthfully,
 For laughter, paraclete of pain,
 Like April suns across the rain.[10]

Sayers was only twenty-two years old when she published this poem, and in the subsequent years of her life, she experienced many trials and heartaches that she probably never imagined when she wrote the poem. Through them all, however, Sayers maintained both her deep commitment to her friends and her ability "to view the whole world mirthfully." She approached life with exuberant joy and used that joy not only to help draw together a host of faithful friends but also to build and maintain various communities that provided her with the emotional and intellectual support that she, as well as the others in the community, needed to create excellent work.

The Joy of Comradeship

Sayers discovered early in her life that she flourished within community. As Barbara Reynolds relates, Sayers's best experiences as a student at Oxford were "the joy of comradeship in organizing and acting a play, the glory of singing with the Bach Choir, and the creative stimulus of exchanging and discussing poetry with fellow enthusiasts."[11] Here, Sayers also discovered that she had a masterful ability to pull a community together through sheer silliness. For example, she once dressed up as Hugh Allen, the director of the Bach choir, for a play that she and some of her friends created. Sayers was generally willing to dress up for a good cause, and often that cause was to help her friends come together as a community through laughter and fun.

---

[10]Sayers, "Hymn," 78.
[11]Barbara Reynolds, *Dorothy L. Sayers: Her Life and Soul* (New York: St. Martin's, 1993), 69.

Figure 11. Marianne the chicken making a fuss

This humor served her well a number of years later when she became one of the founding members of the Detection Club. This club, which is still in existence today, was designed to bring writers of detective fiction together not only to socialize but also to talk shop and hone their craft. From the beginning, this community was held together by a bit of silliness, for all new members were required to participate in

Dorothy L. Sayers's Vision for Communities of Joy

Figure 12. Sayers impersonating the director of the Bach choir

an elaborate initiation ceremony, which included an oath where they promised, among other things, that their "detectives shall well and truly detect the crimes presented to them, using those wits . . . bestow[ed] upon them and not placing reliance on nor mak[ing] use of Divine Revelation, Feminine Intuition, Mumbo-Jumbo, Jiggery Pokery, Coincidence or the Act of God."[12] And after affirming this oath, they were warned, "If you fail to keep your promise, may other writers anticipate your plots, may your publishers do you down in your contracts, may strangers sue you for libel, may your pages swarm with misprints and may your sales continually diminish. Amen."[13] It is suspected that Sayers had a hand in writing the oath, and she certainly took part in the ceremonies, first as the secretary of the club and then as president.

---

[12]"Detection Club Oath," in *The Art of the Mystery Story: A Collection of Critical Essays*, ed. Howard Haycraft (New York: Simon and Schuster, 1947), 198.
[13]"Oath," 199.

The current Detection Club president, Martin Edwards, vividly describes what another ceremony, the installation of a new president, looked like from the perspective of a visitor:

> All of a sudden, the lights went out, plunging the room into darkness. . . . Without warning, a door swung open. The Orator had arrived.
>
> Resplendent in scarlet and black robes, and wearing pince-nez, a statuesque woman entered the room. She marched towards the lectern, holding a single taper to light the way. . . . Stern and purposeful, the Orator lit a candle. . . . At her command, a sombre procession of men and women in evening dress filed into the room. . . . Four members of the group carried flaming torches. Others clutched lethal weapons: a rope, a blunt instrument, a sword, and a phial of poison. A giant of a man brought up the rear. On the cushion that he carried, beneath a black cloth, squatted a grinning human skull. . . . The Orator cleared her throat and began to speak. She administered a lengthy oath to a burly man in his sixties. . . . As the ritual approached its end, the Orator lifted her revolver. Giving a faint smile, she fired a single shot. In the enclosed space, the noise was deafening. Her colleagues let out blood-curdling cries and waved their weapons in the air.
>
> The eyes of the skull lit up the blackness, shining with a fierce red glow.[14]

The Orator in this ceremony was, of course, Dorothy Sayers. Whether she was impersonating her choir director or orchestrating the dramatic initiation rites of the Detection Club, Sayers fully committed herself to the silliness of it all, embracing the "joy of comradeship" in these communities of friends.

---

[14] Martin Edwards, *The Golden Age of Murder* (New York: Harper Collins, 2015), 4-5.

Sayers, in fact, repeatedly gravitated toward communities that combined the seriousness of hard work with the fun of celebrating together, communities that seemed to become even more important in the years following World War I. As Edwards argues, the Detection Club arose at a time when many other groups also began to devote themselves to fun and silliness, for "after the loss of millions of lives in combat, and then during the Spanish flu epidemic [of 1918], games offered escape from the horrors of wartime—as well as from the bleak realities of peace."[15] The Detection Club offered a place where these writers could come together to escape the challenges of their own lives and to share ideas about the works that they were creating, works that would help their readers escape as well.

Figure 13. Eric the Skull

As a writer of detective fiction, Sayers was quite serious about studying her craft and working to develop the genre so that the novels would be more than just intricate puzzles, but she also recognized the simple fun of escapism involved in the stories and never took herself or her works too seriously. She even admonishes some of her critics for their inability to have fun with the stories. In a letter to George Every, for instance, she remarks,

---

[15]Edwards, *Golden Age*, 7.

> These people all sound so cross—as if they wore frightfully scratchy woollies and were in a perpetual state of suppressed irritation. . . . I think there is somewhere in [them] . . . a strong puritanical strain which is fretted by the sight of people enjoying themselves: "Go and see what the children are doing and tell them to stop it at once." That kind of attitude *must* issue in aridity, don't you think? Fertility does call for a certain careless zest and exuberance, and a willingness to rejoice with them that do rejoice.[16]

Sayers certainly had that "exuberance" and "willingness to rejoice with them that do rejoice" in her own life, and she was generally happy to cultivate that in her readers as well as she built her community of loyal fans.

With the outbreak of World War II, Sayers did start to have some misgivings about the escapism of detective fiction that she expresses in *The Mind of the Maker* where she warns her readers that they cannot treat the complexities of real life like the simple problems found in detective stories. But that did not stop her from publishing letters from various characters from her novels to keep up morale during the war, nor did it stop her from continuing to have fun with her detective, Lord Peter Wimsey, even after she stopped writing detective stories. In her essay "Gaudy Night" she confesses:

> Alas! I can now see no end to Peter this side of the grave. . . . His affairs are more real to me than my own. . . . My friends have become infected with my own madness; they wrestle valiantly with dates and genealogical trees and armorial bearings; they assist me to write spoof pamphlets about eighteenth-century

---

[16]Dorothy L. Sayers, *Letter to George Every, July 28, 1947* (Dorothy L. Sayers Papers, Folder 372. The Marion E. Wade Center, Wheaton College, Wheaton, IL).

Dorothy L. Sayers's Vision for Communities of Joy

Wimseys... they accept the existence of a poetical Wimsey who was a friend of Sir Philip Sidney, and meekly sit down to set his songs to music, while the local chemist prepares ink from an Elizabethan recipe wherewith I may forge the original manuscripts in a fair secretary hand. We discover Wimsey ciphers embedded in the plays of Shakespeare, and retrieve Wimsey common-place books from remote corners of Australia; we sally forth in a team to foist these discoveries upon bewildered literary societies in respectable universities.[17]

Sayers fully understood the necessity of addressing the real challenges of her society, and she did so in many of her essays. But she also recognized the importance of embracing a spirit of joy even in the midst of difficulties, and she relished the moments when that joy overflowed into fun, seeing it both as a way to survive amid the challenges of life and as a way to build community with other like-minded people.

Sayers also believed that fun could be a powerful way to help the public engage with more serious issues. In her later detective novels like *Gaudy Night*, for instance, the mysteries are intertwined with important themes such as the value of maintaining integrity in the work a person feels called to do. But it is truly with her work on Dante that Sayers fully embraced the challenge of combining a sense of fun with deep Christian truth. Sayers began reading Dante in an air-raid shelter in 1944, and she was immediately captivated. She expresses her initial excitement about Dante in a letter to Charles Williams, declaring, "I was prepared to find him a GREAT POET, and, of course, a GREAT RELIGIOUS POET, all in solemn capital letters; but I was not prepared to find him good company, and I was

---

[17]Dorothy L. Sayers, "Gaudy Night," in *The Art of the Mystery Story: A Collection of Critical Essays,* ed. Howard Haycraft (New York: Simon and Schuster, 1947), 220-21.

certainly not prepared to find myself continually saying with a chuckle, 'Dear, funny Dante!'"[18] Sayers had expected to find profound theological reflection in Dante's works, but she had not expected to find it conveyed with such humor. She had found a kindred spirit in this writer that she dubbed "the supreme poet of joy,"[19] so she eagerly entered the challenge of translating the *Divine Comedy* for modern readers.

Sayers was convinced that Dante's portrayal of sin and salvation was precisely what an audience needed to read in the years following World War II as they attempted to rebuild their society, and she believed that she could draw them to his seemingly complex poetry by conveying its energy and humor in a new translation. She declares, "If we know how to read [the *Divine Comedy*], we shall find that it has an enormous relevance both to us as individuals and to the world situation to-day."[20] And for Sayers, part of knowing how to read Dante properly meant being able to experience his humor, which she believed had been "hopelessly obscured by his translators and critics."[21] Fully believing in Dante's "dry and delicate and satirical" wit that she compares to Jane Austen's,[22] Sayers set out in her translation to try to convey this "spirit of comedy."[23] Sayers's newly discovered love of Dante brought her, at the end of her life, into a new community with Charles Williams, Barbara Reynolds, and other Dante scholars and students. Through her translation, she worked to bring the common reader into that community as well, not only so that

---

[18]Sayers, *Letters*, 3:77.
[19]Dorothy L. Sayers, introduction to *The Divine Comedy I: Hell*, by Dante Alighieri, trans. Dorothy L. Sayers (New York: Penguin, 1949), 50.
[20]Sayers, introduction to *Divine Comedy*, 9.
[21]Sayers, introduction to *Divine Comedy*, 62.
[22]Sayers, introduction to *Divine Comedy*, 62.
[23]Sayers, introduction to *Divine Comedy*, 64.

they would enjoy the *Divine Comedy* but also so that they would learn from Dante's wisdom.

Throughout her life, Sayers placed herself in communities of kindred spirits who combined the hard work of writing with a spirit of joy, a stance that seemed particularly necessary in the difficult years when her society was recovering first from World War I and then from World War II. This stance was also necessary for Sayers herself as she struggled with the various challenges that arose in her personal life. God may have given Sayers the ability "to view the whole world mirthfully," but He did not exempt her from the difficulties of life: the trials of finding a job that would pay the rent, the pain of several difficult relationships, and the challenge of supporting a son who was born outside of marriage. As a Christian, Sayers knew the power of God's love, faithfulness, and forgiveness, but she still experienced many trials in her life. And as Reynolds recounts in her biography, Sayers struggled at times to find a way out of depression and back into community as well as into joy.[24]

THE DEVELOPMENT OF HARRIET VANE: RECONNECTING WITH COMMUNITY

When we turn to Sayers's detective novels, we can see a fictionalized version of this process. With the character of Harriet Vane, who shares some important qualities with her creator, Sayers powerfully illustrates how difficult it may be not only to reconnect with community but also to find joy within that community. We must, of course, not oversimplify the connection between Sayers and her character, for Harriet is not simply a fictionalized version of Sayers. They are, in fact, quite different in a number of ways. But the fact that Sayers creates

---

[24]Reynolds, *Dorothy L. Sayers*, 129-39.

Harriet as a writer of detective fiction, gives her a tragic love affair that draws on aspects of Sayers's relationships, and anchors her recovery firmly in the academic world of Oxford (which Sayers herself loved) suggests that Sayers may be using Harriet to explore this process of reconnecting with community and joy that was so important in her own life.

Sayers introduces Harriet in the novel *Strong Poison*, which, as I discussed in my first essay, is the novel in which Sayers's detective, Lord Peter Wimsey, comes to truly value community as he relies on his friends and their expertise to help solve the murder and save Harriet, the woman he loves, from being executed for a crime she did not commit. Interestingly, in her essay "Gaudy Night," Sayers explains why she decided to bring a love interest into her detective series despite having condemned that practice in earlier essays. She declares, "Let me confess that when I undertook *Strong Poison* it was with the infanticidal intention of doing away with Peter; that is, of marrying him off and getting rid of him."[25] Sayers does not end the series with *Strong Poison*, however. In fact, she writes six more novels featuring Peter, and in three of these novel she combines the detective story with the development of Peter and Harriet's relationship. She explains this decision by saying, "I could not marry Peter off to the young woman he had ... rescued from death and infamy, because I could find no form of words in which she could accept him without loss of self-respect."[26] Sayers therefore begins to develop both Peter and Harriet in her subsequent novels, rounding out Peter's character so that he could become more of "a complete human being" and tracing Harriet's development as she recovers from the devastating experience of being

---

[25]Sayers, "Gaudy Night," 210.
[26]Sayers, "Gaudy Night," 211.

on trial for murder.[27] This process is a fascinating one, and a number of scholars have explored what Sayers is saying about love, integrity, marriage, and gender roles through her development of this relationship.[28] But what I find particularly interesting is that Harriet grows not only in her ability to respect herself and admit her love for Peter but also in her ability to enter into community and experience joy. The trajectory of the four novels that feature Harriet and Peter's relationship moves not only toward the joy of marriage but also toward the joy of community, powerfully illustrating both the importance that Sayers placed on community and the essential quality of joy that she believes may be found within it.

At the beginning of *Strong Poison*, Harriet is completely alienated from community. Our first glimpse of her comes as she stands alone facing the judge who is summarizing the case against her. She is introduced only as "the prisoner... [whose] eyes, like dark smudges under the heavy square brows, seemed equally without fear and without hope."[29] This sense of alienation and isolation is emphasized later when Peter visits Harriet in prison and is given the procedures that he

---

[27]Sayers, "Gaudy Night," 211.
[28]See Laura K. Ray's "The Mysteries of *Gaudy Night*: Feminism, Faith, and the Depths of Character," in *Mystery and Detection Annual* (1973): 272-85; Margaret P. Hannay's "Harriet's Influence on the Characterization of Lord Peter Wimsey," in *As Her Whimsey Took Her: Critical Essays on the Work of Dorothy L. Sayers*, ed. Margaret P. Hannay (Kent, OH: Kent State University Press, 1979), 36-50; Carolyn G. Hart's "*Gaudy Night*: Quintessential Sayers," in *Dorothy L. Sayers: The Centenary Celebration*, ed. Alzina Stone Dale (New York: Walker, 1993), 45-50; B. J. Rahn's "The Marriage of True Minds," in *Dorothy L. Sayers: The Centenary Celebration*, ed. Alzina Stone Dale (New York: Walker, 1993), 50-65; as well as my articles "'Detachment Is a Rare Virtue': Dorothy L. Sayers and the Construction of Female Identity," in *Persona and Paradox: Issues of Identity for C. S. Lewis, His Friends and Associates*, ed. Suzanne Bray and William Gray (Newcastle upon Tyne, UK: Cambridge Scholars, 2012), 156-67; "Dorothy L. Sayers and the Theology of Gender," in *Christianity and the Detective Story*, ed. Anya Morlan and Walter Raubicheck (Newcastle upon Tyne, UK: Cambridge Scholars, 2013), 87-102.
[29]Dortothy L. Sayers, *Strong Poison* (New York: Harper, 1995), 1.

must follow during the visit. The warder explains, "You sit at one end and the prisoner at the other, and you must be careful not to move from your seats, nor to pass any object over the table. I shall be outside and see you through the glass."[30] As a prisoner, Harriet has lost the freedom to communicate freely with others and enter into community with them, and as much as Peter tries to break down that barrier in their meetings, he can never manage to truly connect with Harriet, who, while appreciating the work he does to prove her innocence, repeatedly refuses to marry him.

As Sayers illustrates, however, Harriet's feelings of alienation go much deeper than this, for Harriet had isolated herself from community even before she was accused of murdering her lover, Philip Boyes. As one of the witnesses relates during the trial, "Harriet Vane obviously felt her unfortunate position [of living with a man outside of marriage] very acutely—cutting herself off from her family friends and refusing to thrust herself into company where her social outlawry might cause embarrassment."[31] Sayers emphasizes the depth of this isolation even further by revealing that even Bohemian London, the one community that does not condemn Harriet for her decision, is not a very welcoming place for her. While a couple of the women from this community support her during the trial, most are so consumed with their own lives that they cannot be bothered to think about anyone else, and some are actively hostile, believing that Harriet murdered Boyes out of "beastly spite and jealousy."[32] And as if this isolation were not bad enough, Sayers takes it one step further by revealing the loneliness that Harriet experienced even within her relationship with

---

[30]*SP*, 41.
[31]*SP*, 5.
[32]*SP*, 85.

Boyes, for when Peter asks Harriet if she was friends with Boyes, she replies, "'No.' The word broke out with a kind of repressed savagery that startled him. 'Philip wasn't the sort of man to make a friend of a woman.'"[33] Harriet's experience of being accused of murder certainly increases her sense of isolation, but as Sayers portrays it, this isolation began long before her arrest and has had a powerful effect on her.

In one of the conversations that Sayers crafts between Peter and Harriet, she reveals just how much Harriet has been damaged by her isolation. After Peter humorously recounts his feelings after an ill-fated love affair, they have the following exchange:

> "If anybody ever marries you, it will be for the pleasure of hearing you talk piffle," said Harriet severely.
> "A humiliating reason, but better than no reason at all."
> "I used to talk piffle rather well myself," said Harriet, with tears in her eyes, "but it's got knocked out of me. You know—I was really meant to be a cheerful person—all this gloom and suspicion isn't the real me. But I've lost my nerve somehow."[34]

Harriet's experiences have deadened her ability to enjoy the silly fun of talking piffle or nonsense, but even more than that they have deadened her ability to experience the deeper joy of community that is built as friends engage in piffle. You cannot talk piffle alone. You need friends not only to appreciate it but also to respond in kind. As this novel concludes, the ramifications of Harriet's pain are clear, for she is unable to return to community. Upon her acquittal, she simply desires "to get out of this and be left alone."[35] Harriet wishes only for deeper isolation, and as Sayers demonstrates through the next three

---
[33]*SP*, 43.
[34]*SP*, 128-29.
[35]*SP*, 246.

novels, Harriet's sense of joy and fun is restored not simply by eventually marrying Peter but also by being integrated into strong, nurturing communities.

With *Have His Carcase*, Sayers begins to explore the complexities of Harriet's recovery, a recovery which, while having its positives (a focus on "honest work" and "physical activity"), also has its negatives (a continuing isolation as she embarks on a "solitary walking tour").[36] Peter, in fact, diagnoses the essence of Harriet's struggle, declaring, "You don't want ever again to have to depend for happiness on another person," to which Harriet responds, "That's true. That's the truest thing you ever said."[37] Harriet fears entering into a relationship with anyone, and Sayers highlights these fears with the setting she creates for this mystery. The dead man that Harriet discovers on the beach during her walking tour turns out to be a dancer at the Resplendent Hotel in the seaside resort of Wilvercombe, and as Harriet begins to investigate the case, she discovers the pathetic desperation that lies just beneath the surface of this community. Upon entering the ballroom of the hotel, Harriet notices the absurd roles everyone enacts as the professional dancers try to attract the attention of the wealthy guests, and the guests try to relive their youth. She is particularly struck by "a lean woman, pathetically made up, dressed in an exaggeration of the fashion which it would have been difficult for a girl of nineteen to carry off successfully."[38] As it turns out, this woman, Mrs. Weldon, is engaged to one of the dancers, Paul Alexis, who is, in fact, the man whose body Harriet discovered on the beach. With her desperate (and rather ridiculous) love for Paul, a young man who made his living by

---

[36]Dorothy L. Sayers, *Have His Carcase* (New York: Harper, 1995), 1.
[37]*HHC*, 168.
[38]*HHC*, 38.

flattering wealthy, older women, Mrs. Weldon, like most of the members of this community, is caught up in an illusion of love, making this community particularly problematic for Harriet's recovery. Not only does it repeatedly remind Harriet of her own mistake of devoting herself to a man who did not truly love her and whom she did not love either, but it also increases her fears of entering a relationship again.

Sayers reveals these fears even more fully through the way she develops Harriet and Peter's relationship in this novel. On the surface, they begin to develop rapport as they investigate the mystery together, but underneath Harriet is still consumed with bitterness over her past and resentment against Peter. This becomes painfully clear in a scene where they initially seem to be caught up in the fun of figuring out the clues to the mystery. That mood is quickly broken when Harriet lists herself as one of the suspects and declares,

> You thought I was pretty brazen, when you found me getting publicity out of the thing [discovering the body]. So I was. There's no choice for a person like me to be anything but brazen.... But do you think it makes matters any more agreeable to know that it is only the patronage of Lord Peter Wimsey that prevent men like [the inspector] from being openly hostile? ... I suppose you think I haven't been humiliated enough already, without this parade of chivalry.[39]

Harriet cannot escape her notoriety. She resents being placed once again in the position of having to be grateful for Peter's assistance, and she refuses to let that gratitude compel her into a relationship.

In fact, the entire episode makes them uncomfortable. At the end of the novel, Peter reflects, "Well ... isn't that a damned awful, bitter,

---

[39] *HHC*, 165-66.

bloody farce? The old fool who wanted a lover and the young fool who wanted an empire. One throat cut and three people hanged. . . . I always did hate watering-places!"[40] Interestingly, Peter concludes by indicting not just the crime but also the community. With this line, which is actually the final line of the novel, Sayers reminds her readers of the dangers that have flourished in the false community of this resort, and she sets the stage for the type of community that she creates for Harriet in the next novel, *Gaudy Night*. It is in this novel that Harriet experiences a better community that eventually allows her to recover the sense of joy that has been lacking in both *Strong Poison* and *Have His Carcase*.

In *Gaudy Night* Sayers completes the process by which Harriet and Peter are finally able to come together. Harriet, by returning to Oxford to investigate a series of crimes at her old college, immerses herself in the integrity of the scholarly life and rediscovers her self-worth, and Peter develops the humility and vulnerability that allow Harriet to envision the possibility of an equal relationship with him. Their love story permeates the novel, but, significantly, Peter and Harriet's union comes about only when they have reconnected to the community of Oxford, which, while certainly not perfect, is revealed to be a far better community than the world of Bohemian London that we saw in *Strong Poison* or the world of the Resplendent Hotel in *Have His Carcase*. With this novel, Sayers asks her readers to revel in the joy of these characters finally coming together, but she also asks her readers to recognize that this joy becomes possible because the relationship is nurtured within the joy of the wider community of Oxford.

Sayers emphasizes the importance of this communal sense of joy with the title of the novel. *Gaudy* comes from the Latin *gaudium*,

---

[40]*HHC*, 440.

which means "joy" or "delight," and it is the name given to college reunions at Oxford when the graduates return for a weekend to revel in the joys that they once experienced within the community of their college. The novel, in fact, begins with Harriet considering whether or not to return to Shrewsbury College for the "Gaudy." A friend has asked her to attend, but she is hesitant to go. She reflects,

> It was... so long ago; so closely encompassed and complete; so cut off as by swords from the bitter years that lay between. Could one face it now? What would those women say to her, to Harriet Vane, who had taken her first in English and gone to London to write mystery fiction, to live with a man who was not married to her, and to be tried for his murder amid a roar of notoriety? That was not the kind of career that Shrewsbury expected of its old students.[41]

While several years have passed since her trial, Harriet's first impulse is still to isolate herself. She is afraid of how she will be received by others and does not wish to tarnish her wonderful memories of university.

She decides to attend, however, and it is at the Gaudy that she receives a brief glimmer of the joy she longs to recapture, a joy that comes, significantly, by being in community. As she listens to one of the speeches at the Gaudy dinner, she imagines "that whole wildly heterogeneous, that even slightly absurd collection of chattering women fused into a corporate unity with one another and with every man and woman to whom integrity of mind meant more than material gain."[42] She then comes to the realization that "in the glamour of one Gaudy night, one could realize that one was a citizen of no mean city. It might be an old and old-fashioned city, with inconvenient buildings

---

[41] Dorothy L. Sayers, *Gaudy Night* (New York: Harper, 1995), 2.
[42] *GN*, 29.

and narrow streets... but her foundations were set upon the holy hills and her spires touched heaven."[43] As she listens, Harriet begins to recognize in herself an integrity of mind that would enable her to transcend her past and enter again into this academic community, reflecting, "To be true to one's calling, whatever follies one might commit in one's emotional life, that was the way to spiritual peace."[44] And with these reflections, she begins the process of rediscovering her self-worth. This "Gaudy night," which Sayers emphasizes with her title, begins Harriet's quest to once again experience the joy of being part of a community.

Sayers continues to emphasize Harriet's quest for joy within community with the mystery that Harriet is tasked with solving. Harriet's search for the poison pen writer who threatens the peace and security of Shrewsbury College repeatedly compels her to reflect on whether this academic community truly has the integrity and joy that she so desperately desires. Even before she is asked to investigate the crimes, Harriet has some misgivings about her college. She is warmly welcomed by Miss Martin, the Dean, who encourages her not to worry about her past, saying, "Nobody bothers about it at all,"[45] and by Miss Lydgate, her former tutor, who "spoke appreciatively of her work, and commended her for keeping up a scholarly standard of English, even in mystery fiction."[46] Yet she also receives an anonymous note stating, "YOU DIRTY MURDERESS. AREN'T YOU ASHAMED TO SHOW YOUR FACE?"[47] Upon receiving the note, Harriet cries, "Oxford, thou too?"[48] and begins to wonder whether this community is just as flawed

---

[43] GN, 29.
[44] GN, 29.
[45] GN, 10.
[46] GN, 16.
[47] GN, 58.
[48] GN, 58.

as the rest of the world, a supposition that only increases as she begins her investigation.

When Harriet moves into the college upon being asked to investigate the source of the nasty letters and vandalism that have been plaguing the residents, she begins to wonder about the health of this community. Harriet loves the commitment to scholarly excellence that she sees in dons such as Miss Lydgate and Miss De Vine, and she herself revels in it as she does her own research on the mystery writer Sheridan Le Fanu. She also admires the compassion that these women have for everyone in the community. Hearing about their care for one of the retired servants, she "marveled, not for the first time, at the untiring conscientiousness of administrative women. Nobody's interests ever seemed to be overlooked or forgotten, and an endless goodwill made up for a perennial scarcity of funds."[49] Harriet herself experiences this compassion as various dons provide her with counsel and support during her time at the college. Her joy of returning to this community, however, is tempered by the crimes that she observes, which cause her to question not only the individual women who make up the community but also the entire premise of this secluded, academic world. She reflects, "The warped and repressed mind is apt enough to turn and wound itself. 'Soured virginity'—'unnatural life'— 'semi-demented spinsters'—'starved appetites and suppressed impulses'— 'unwholesome atmosphere'—she could think of whole sets of epithets, ready-minted for circulation. Was this what lived in the tower set on the hill?"[50] Harriet begins to wonder which one of the students or dons could be the warped mind behind the crimes, and she feels torn between her desire to enter into this "quiet place" where she may

---
[49]GN, 44.
[50]GN, 77-78.

recover her sense of worth and integrity and her fears that the community will disappoint her.[51]

With the conclusion of the mystery, in which Peter is able to prove that the acts were not committed by the dons or the students, Sayers once again affirms the value of this community as Harriet reflects, "They were all normal again. They had never been anything else. Now that the distorting-glass of suspicion was removed, they were kindly, intelligent human beings . . . as understandable and pleasant as daily bread."[52] These women are not perfect by any means. As Janice Brown remarks, "There is a continual smoldering of petty jealousy and unpleasant competitiveness among the dons."[53] But, as Brown also acknowledges, there is "brilliant intellect and noble character . . . [and] there is a depth of sensitivity and compassion."[54] At the end of the novel, Shrewsbury College has become a model of the type of community that Sayers values, a community where everyone is committed not only to the integrity of her work but also to the support of the other members. By immersing herself in this community, Harriet is finally able to recover from her past trauma, regain the integrity that she felt she had lost during her relationship with Boyes, and experience the joy of being in a community of friends.

Sayers continues to emphasize the importance of this community by the way she finally brings Peter and Harriet together. Harriet initially worries that by asking for Peter's help with this mystery "she had called in something explosive from the outside world to break up the ordered tranquility of the place," but she realizes almost immediately

---

[51]*GN*, 17.
[52]*GN*, 493.
[53]Janice Brown, *The Seven Deadly Sins in the Work of Dorothy L. Sayers* (Kent, OH: Kent State University Press, 1998), 157.
[54]Brown, *Seven Deadly Sins*, 164.

"that the image had been a false one. [Peter] came into the quiet room as though he belonged there, and had never belonged to any other place."⁵⁵ Like Harriet, Peter, as a graduate of Balliol College, returns to Oxford as a part of that community, and he values it for exactly the same reasons that Harriet does. He tells her, "Here's where real things are done.... If only one could root one's self in here among the grass and stones and do something worth doing."⁵⁶ For the first time, Harriet realizes that she and Peter, who because of class differences and the scandal of her trial have seemed to exist in entirely different realms, can be part of the same community. Peter recognizes it as well. As they stand together on the Radcliffe Camera surveying the towers of the various colleges, he tells her, "I set out in a lordly manner to offer you heaven and earth. I find that all I have to give you is Oxford—which was yours already."⁵⁷ The joy that Peter and Harriet experience as Harriet finally accepts Peter's proposal is fully immersed in the joy that both have already experienced within the community of Oxford, for it is their commitment to the integrity of this community that finally allows them to come together as equals.

Sayers powerfully illustrates how firmly embedded this relationship is in the community of Oxford by the way that she orchestrates the scene in which Harriet finally agrees to marry Peter. In this scene, both are dressed in academic robes, and Peter's proposal follows the form used in Oxford to confirm academic degrees. He asks, *"Placetne, magistra?"* [Does it please (thee), mistress?], and she replies, *"Placet"* (it pleases).⁵⁸ While the passing Procter is scandalized to see "Senior Members of the University ... passionately embracing in New College

---
⁵⁵*GN*, 305.
⁵⁶*GN*, 307.
⁵⁷*GN*, 497.
⁵⁸*GN*, 501.

Lane,"[59] readers are not. It seems entirely appropriate that this moment of joy for Peter and Harriet is wrapped up in their identities as members of the university, for, as Sayers has revealed throughout the novel, this "Gaudy night" has become possible because of the initial "Gaudy night" that helped Harriet begin to reconnect with the community of Oxford. Ultimately, Harriet's joy in this academic community enables the healing that allows her to commit to a relationship with Peter.

In her final novel, *Busman's Honeymoon*, Sayers continues to emphasize the importance of this sense of joy in community as she explores the early days of Peter and Harriet's marriage.[60] In this novel, Sayers presents the couple with a number of challenges to their relationship that they must negotiate as they investigate the murder of a man found in the basement of their new home. Will their love for each other corrupt their judgment? Will their relationship withstand Peter's guilt over the results of the investigation? The process is not an easy one, for as Miss de Vine warned Harriet in *Gaudy Night*, "A marriage of two independent and equally irritable intelligences seems . . . reckless to the point of insanity. You can hurt one another so dreadfully."[61] But they are able to grow and adapt. And by concluding the novel with a selection from John Donne's poem, "Eclogue for the Marriage of the Earl of Somerset," Sayers suggests that, by the end, they are able to achieve "joy's bonfire . . . where love's strong arts / Make of so noble individual parts / One fire of four inflaming eyes, and of two

---

[59]*GN*, 501.
[60]The value that Sayers placed on community is also emphasized in a different way at the beginning of *Busman's Honeymoon*, where she includes a letter to her friends Muriel St. Clare Byrne, Helen Simpson, and Marjorie Barber, thanking them for all the support they provided as she crafted the story.
[61]*GN*, 492.

loving hearts."[62] The focus of this novel is truly on the development of their relationship that leads them to this "joy's bonfire," but once again Sayers positions that joy within the context of the wider communities that Harriet is finally willing to enter into, showing just how far she has moved from the isolation of *Strong Poison*.

Sayers highlights the importance of community right from the beginning of this novel, for it opens not with Peter and Harriet's reflections on their marriage but rather with comments from other members of their community, such as Peter's mother, Miss Martin (the Dean of Shrewsbury College), and Bunter (Peter's manservant). Through this, Sayers draws attention to the people who surround and support Peter and Harriet in their marriage. Sayers also draws attention to this supportive community by including the comments of one outsider, Helen, Peter's snobbish sister-in-law, who strongly conveys her distaste for the odd assortment of people who attend the wedding. Helen recounts that Harriet is "married from a Woman's College"[63] and is "attended by the most incredible assortment of bridesmaids—all female dons!—and an odd, dark woman to give her away, who was supposed to be the Head of the College."[64] And Peter has gathered "all kinds of queer people in the church ... that ridiculous old Climpson woman, and some hangers-on that [he] had picked up in the course of his 'cases,' and several policemen."[65] There is even "a man in a Salvation Army uniform, who ... was a retired burglar."[66] While Helen is appalled, readers recognize how appropriate it is for Harriet and Peter to be married surrounded by their unique assortment of friends. As Sayers

---

[62]Dorothy L. Sayers, *Busman's Honeymoon* (New York: Harper, 1995), 403.
[63]*BH*, 6.
[64]*BH*, 7.
[65]*BH*, 7.
[66]*BH*, 7.

reminds us, Harriet and Peter are not simply marrying each other; they are also entering each other's communities, as odd as those communities may seem to others.

Harriet herself realizes the significance of this when she considers the important role that Bunter has played in Peter's life and the close connection that they have. Early in the novel, the narrator tells us that Harriet "felt horribly guilty about Bunter and hoped his feelings weren't going to be hurt, because if he gave notice it would break Peter's heart,"[67] and later Harriet tells Peter directly, "though he's charming to me, our marriage must have been an awful blow to him."[68] Harriet recognizes that by marrying Peter she is also entering this close-knit community that has existed for many years without her, and throughout the novel, she often turns to Bunter for advice, knowing that in certain respects, he knows Peter far better than she does. True to form, Bunter takes everything in stride, fully accepting Harriet's new position in the community, a point that Sayers highlights in Bunter's letter to his mother, in which he remarks, "We were happily married this morning."[69]

Sayers intensifies this focus on community for Harriet even further with her choice of the honeymoon destination. To evade the prying eyes of the press, Peter and Harriet escape to the home that they recently purchased in the small, rural community where Harriet grew up. For Harriet, the woman who cut herself off entirely from her previous life when she lived with Boyes, the decision to return to this community is significant, for she is essentially returning home, embracing it as the place where she wishes to begin her married life. And

---

[67] *BH*, 15.
[68] *BH*, 301.
[69] *BH*, 8.

she makes no secret of her connection, introducing herself as "Dr. Vane's daughter, that used to live at Great Pagford."[70] Now that she is rooted in the community created by her marriage, she also wishes to reconnect with the community of her childhood, and just as she discovered with the academic community of Oxford, Peter fits perfectly within this community as well. As Harriet watches Peter interact with the vicar, she reflects, "[Peter] belonged to an ordered society, and this was it. More than any of the friends in her own world, he spoke the familiar language of her childhood."[71] To emphasize this point, Sayers has Peter, responding to the vicar's invitation to a concert, break into song to be joined first by Harriet, then by Mr. Puffett (the chimney sweep), Mr. Goodacre (the vicar), and Miss Twitterton (the church organist). By having this odd assortment of characters come together quite literally in harmony, Sayers not only illustrates the ease with which both Peter and Harriet enter this world but also reveals just how much Harriet has changed over the course of the novels. We finally see her happy and truly at ease as she returns to her childhood community. She is even able to engage in piffle as she, Peter, and the Superintendent trade literary quotations back and forth during the investigation.

Sayers emphasizes just how much Harriet has changed in a conversation that she crafts between Peter and Harriet in which Peter asks Harriet if she finds life "worth living."[72] In response, Harriet declares, "Yes! I've always felt absolutely certain it was good—if only one could get it straightened out. I've hated almost everything that ever happened to me, but I *knew* all the time it was just things that were wrong, not everything."[73] She then reflects on how her life has changed: "It seems

---

[70]*BH*, 40.
[71]*BH*, 98.
[72]*BH*, 261.
[73]*BH*, 262.

like a miracle to be able to look forward—to—to see all the minutes in front of one come hopping along with something marvelous in them."[74] Harriet has settled into the joy of her marriage to Peter as well as the joy of a wider community, and this has completely transformed her life. While she had always believed that life was good, she is finally able to experience it as good.

Significantly, it is from this position that Sayers then allows Harriet to help Peter through his own crisis as he begins to isolate himself in response to the repercussions of his investigation. As readers of the series know, Peter often struggles intensely at the conclusion of his cases as he grapples with the realities of what he has done. As his mother describes it, "He doesn't like responsibility, you know . . . the War and one thing and another was bad for people that way."[75] While Peter can hold to his belief in the integrity of his job during the investigation, he has difficulty seeing its value once someone is sentenced to death based on his information, and he worries that he inevitably ends up injuring the community he was trying to help. At the conclusion of *Busman's Honeymoon*, Peter retreats further and further into himself as the time of the execution draws near, and Harriet wonders if he will choose simply to disappear as he has in the past. In her distress, she turns to Bunter, who has much more experience with Peter's moods than she does, and together, they work to provide the support he needs and bring him back into the community of their family. Eventually, Peter returns home to wait out the long hours before the execution with Harriet, and it is here that Harriet helps Peter remember the value of his work to the wider community so that he may once again become part of it.

---

[74] *BH*, 262.
[75] *BH*, 385.

Dorothy L. Sayers's Vision for Communities of Joy

As they discuss Peter's fear about the damage he may have done with the investigation, Harriet reminds him that his commitment to the integrity of his job has enabled him not only to purge evil from this community but also to protect the innocent. She tells him, "If you hadn't meddled, it might have been Joe Sellon or Aggie Twitterton [facing execution]. ... If you hadn't meddled six years ago, it would almost certainly have been me."[76] Harriet, who was drawn back into the community of Oxford by focusing on the integrity of her own work, comforts her husband with the same idea. She helps him recover from his own fears and isolation so that they may reach the "joy's bonfire" of marriage described in John Donne's poem as Peter turns to Harriet in his distress and she "[holds] him, crouched at her knees, against her breast, huddling his head in her arms."[77]

Sayers does not leave the story there, however, for in her short story "Talboys,"[78] she reveals that this healing has implications not simply for Peter and Harriet's marriage but also for their connection to community. In this story, we get a glimpse of the Wimseys just a few years later, and they are firmly and happily rooted back in this community where they have chosen to rear their three sons. Despite the difficulties of the case in *Busman's Honeymoon* and the ease with which they could have relocated and forgotten all about that place, Harriet and Peter decide to return to Harriet's childhood community. This final image of the family happily living within this community is an important one, for it illustrates that with the trajectory of her works, Sayers does far more than simply trace the development of Peter and Harriet's relationship. She embeds it in Harriet's difficult but necessary journey of

---

[76] *BH*, 401.
[77] *BH*, 403.
[78] Dorothy L. Sayers, "Talboys," in *Lord Peter: A Collection of All the Lord Peter Wimsey Stories* (New York: Harper 2013), 451-74.

reconnecting with community and rediscovering joy. In this final story, we see that Harriet has not only recovered from her own grief and isolation but has also helped her husband recover from his, enabling them to rear their children within both a nurturing family and a nurturing community.

By the end of the series, Harriet recovers her sense of joy and becomes the "cheerful person" she was meant to be, and her process for doing so, which was so powerfully affected by the joy she experienced in the intellectual integrity of the academic community of Oxford, is one that certainly resonates with Sayers's own life. As we have seen, Sayers, too, was deeply committed to individuals finding their particular vocations and working in them with integrity. However, Sayers ultimately has an even deeper source for her joy in community than Harriet does. At the conclusion of *Busman's Honeymoon*, Harriet's hope rests primarily on her and Peter's integrity of mind, as she reminds him of all the individuals and communities he has helped to save through his investigations. Readers familiar with the entire series may realize, however, that this integrity of mind does not always result in joyful community. In some cases, as in *Unnatural Death* and *The Nine Tailors*, Peter's investigations actually do have negative repercussions on innocent people and their communities. While integrity of mind may be an important component within community, Sayers recognizes that it may not be the strongest foundation for it.

And it is here, as I conclude this series of essays, that I must return to ideas explored in my first two essays, which give a clearer sense of where Sayers's foundation for joy in community actually lies. As I mentioned in my first essay, at the conclusion of *The Nine Tailors* Sayers provides Peter with a much stronger foundation for hope in the words of Reverend Venables, who responds to Peter's distress over his investigation by remarking, "My dear boy . . . it does not do for us to take too much thought for the morrow. It is better to follow the truth and leave the result in the hand of God. He can foresee where we cannot, because He knows all the facts."[79] While Sayers, like Harriet, is fully committed to truth and integrity of mind, she also believes, like Venables, that God is the only one who can ultimately bring order to the seeming chaos. This reliance on God is essential, for as I explored in my second essay, Sayers recognizes that we, as individuals, are inevitably flawed. As she illustrates in *The Zeal of Thy House* with the character William of Sens, Sayers knows that even our best attempts to work with integrity are never perfect. Sayers has confidence, though, that God has the power not only to purify our motives and perfect our work but also to bring us back into true community. For Sayers, then, joy in community is ultimately possible not because we can see how everything has worked out in the past but rather because we can trust that God will fulfill His perfect work in the future even as He works with flawed individuals and flawed communities.

With this deep foundation for her hope, Sayers herself was able to fully experience the joy that comes both from seeing the "world mirthfully" and from sharing that mirth with good friends. As Reynolds states, "Gaudium, elation of the soul, was a virtue [Sayers] did not find difficult to practice."[80] Sayers found joy in being part of communities of action and doing the good, hard work that she felt called to do. She found joy in being part of a community of faith as she worked to uphold the truths of Christianity while also supporting the good work of her Christian friends and colleagues. And she found joy in her day-to-day interactions with friends as she built

---

[79]Dorothy L. Sayers, *The Nine Tailors*, (New York: Harvest/Harcourt, 1962), 307.
[80]Reynolds, introduction to *Letters*, 3:xvi.

relationships based not only on shared interests and deep truth but also on silly stories about her chickens. Sayers fully embraced the command in Philippians 4:4 to "Rejoice in the Lord always," and she encouraged her community of friends as well as her community of readers to do so also.

RESPONSE

Bryan T. McGraw

My thanks to Christine Colón for her excellent series of essays and especially for the opportunity to respond to this last one on the relation of joy and community. It is worth noting, though, that you might discover at the end of these few pages that you've made a terrible mistake. Three of them, actually. First, I am no literary scholar, and indeed, I only began reading Sayers when I arrived here ten years ago at Wheaton. I am, in the parlance of our age, a noob. Second, I am hardly known as a "joyous" person; indeed, I have long attempted to cultivate a bit of a curmudgeonly reputation, at least among my students and my children—and here, at least, I've had some stunning successes. Third, and a bit more seriously, since I am by vocation a *political* theorist, I am always and everywhere inclined to view things in relation to the relatively jaundiced world of politics. That is, you've invited into your midst an all-too-often grumpy amateur whose instincts are to relate everything to politics. If you want help in viewing the world mirthfully, I may not be much help.

And yet, when Colón sent me a copy of her essays, I was thrilled, for when I first discovered the series of detective novels centered on Lord Peter Death Bredon Wimsey, I devoured them one after another precisely because they were indeed so joyous. Consider, if you will, P. D. James's mystery novels as an interesting contrast. Her most famous character, Adam Dalgliesh, is, like Peter, a master detective and a master of arcane knowledge, especially (in his case) of the visual arts.

But his life is a gloomy struggle. He is, I have sometimes thought, a personification of post-Christian Britain, resplendent with treasures from ages past, still learned, still committed to its duties, and yet slowly dying inside. Not so with Lord Peter: his humor, excitement, love, exuberance, and *joy* radiate through every story. There is also some deep sadness—more on that in a bit—but no one reading these novels could miss what a singularly and profoundly joyful character he is.

So I hope to follow Professor Colón's lead and spend just a few pages reflecting on the relationship between joy and community as exhibited in some of Sayers's detective fiction. Of course, because I am a political theorist I cannot help but ask about the place of joy in the distinctively *political* community (as over against other sorts communities like churches, theater troupes, or detection societies): does the business of legislation, judging, elections, back-room deals, and violence have a place for joy? Our day, perhaps like many others, evinces little if any joy in our politics. We are more apt to suppose that politics requires struggle, calculation, passion, anger, and conflict, or maybe it requires, as the philosophers sometimes pretend, just better rational deliberation. But joy? Hardly.

There is inevitably some truth to this commonplace, for political communities are indeed substantively different than other sorts of communities and thus ask different things of us. To suppose the sort of joy that can inhabit a marriage or a church or a theater troupe can or should also inhabit a political community is probably a mistake. Politics is, to my mind, too tied up with the tragic to ever be constituted by joy in the same way as, say, a marriage might be. But we need not despair; indeed, we should not despair, for while political communities cannot have joy precisely this way, they might be able to grasp hope, perhaps joy's first cousin. This would not be the sort of cheap hope packaged by hucksters and utopians alike but rather a hard-won trust grounded in faith and fully aware of its tragic limits. As much as Sayers provokes us to "view the world mirthfully" in both Peter's exuberance and Harriet's redemption, Professor Colón calls our attention, perhaps, to joy's limits in the context of that community whose intractable characteristic, this side of the eschaton, is in dealing out death. We cannot do without joy. But as Peter in particular shows us, politics—also necessary for our flourishing—carries tragedy in its wake, no matter what those hucksters or utopians may suppose. We should refuse the double temptation, on the one hand, to eschew the tragic and ignore joy's limits and, on the other, to make it all politics and lose joy (and hope) altogether. Or so it seems to me.

I confess that one of the best things about Professor Colón's paper is that it redeems for this reader the character Harriet Vane, who had been one of my least favorite of the characters connected to Peter Wimsey. Her unwillingness to extend to Peter even the most basic elements of gratitude for saving her life in *Strong Poison* had always bothered me. Her persistent brush-off had always struck me as just odd and, frankly, made me dislike her so much that I was even a bit disappointed when I realized that Peter was in love with her and that they were headed to marriage. Professor Colón shows us, though, how Vane's character reveals something important for us, namely the interrelation of joy and community.

When we first meet Harriet, she is both alone and joyless. It is hard to imagine someone of her class being more alone, ostracized for an illicit relationship with Philip Boyes and in prison accused of his murder. Bereft of friends, she cannot seem to even lean on a memory of her relationship with Boyes to sustain her. She is utterly alone, and the idea of "viewing the world mirthfully" seems utterly impossible.

It's easy to see why Harriet, with her lover dead and her own life on the line, would be a bit on the sad side. That seems a normal human response. But even after she is exonerated, she exhibits no joy; she can't even manage relief or gratitude, really. It is only, Professor Colón suggests, with the rediscovery of good community—first at Oxford and then with Peter—that joy returns. Why?

Professor Colón reads Sayers as suggesting that these are places where she comes to be supported and valued, and where she can do good work (both scholarly and detective work). It is only in good community, we might say, that Harriet Vane begins to reacquire her self-respect, her sense that she genuinely belongs and is not just an object of condemnation or curiosity or pity. That all seems right to me: we can't flourish as human beings—and surely joy is a part of human flourishing—outside of our belonging to good communities, places where we are known and valued.

This is a lesson that we late moderns (or maybe postmoderns) have forgotten or missed. I'll not bore you with another jeremiad against individualism—the ubiquity of such calls, especially among Christians, merely demonstrates its power—but surely something is deeply wrong with our society. American life expectancy dropped last year for the second year in a row—the first time it has done that in over fifty years.[1] The biggest change was in deaths from "unintentional injuries" and suicides. That rise in "unintentional injuries" was due, according to the Centers for Disease Control and Prevention, to unintentional drug overdoses—opioids, mostly. It is commonplace now to worry about how large swathes of our country are seized by a kind of existential despair that gives rise to such deaths. Its causes are no doubt numerous: economic stress, family breakdown, social media, reality television, and so on.

---

[1] See Lenny Bernstein and Christopher Ingraham, "Fueled by Drug Crisis, U.S. Life Expectancy Declines for a Second Straight Year," *Washington Post*, December 21, 2017.

Dorothy L. Sayers's Vision for Communities of Joy

But perhaps Harriet Vane's character suggests another reason: our solitude, or maybe more precisely, our lack of community, our lack of real connection to others. Jean Twenge published an article in the September 2017 edition of the *Atlantic Monthly* that parents in my circle have passed around and talked about a lot.[2] Twenge noted that teen behaviors have shifted significantly over the last decade or so: drug use, sexual activity, auto accidents, and the like have all fallen dramatically. But rates of anxiety, depression, and suicide have risen just as dramatically. The culprit, she suggests, is the smartphone, that handheld computer, phone, camera, and television all-in-one that offers us the *simulacra* of connection without the real, physical, tangible presence of another human person. Perhaps one way to put it—and I don't know if Professor Twenge would put it this way, but I think Professor Colón would—is that we suffer, as Harriet Vane suffered, from a lack of genuine friendship. Yes, she lacked community, but it would be more exact to say that she lacked *good* or *real* community. But it would even be better to say that she lacked friends. Friends, as we just learned, let us talk "piffle," allow us to extend beyond ourselves, be silly, be valued, be known. When we think about why Harriet Vane has no joy, the most straightforward (and maybe deepest) answer is because she has no friends.

Peter, of course, is just the opposite. He has friends all over the place, which is one reason I had always found Harriet's rebuff so striking. Aside from criminals and other louts, who wouldn't want to be friends with Peter Wimsey? He's always up to one thing or another, he's tremendously generous and kind, and he just radiates an exuberance that is altogether childlike (in the best sense of the term). He takes joy in

---

[2]Jean Twenge, "Have Smartphones Destroyed a Generation?" *The Atlantic Monthly*, September 2017.

his work, and that joy draws quite the motley—and deeply loyal—crew to him. But as Professor Colón notes, he is also at times deeply melancholic. Throughout the full series, we get hints that he carries serious psychological scars from his wartime service and (before he meets Harriet) from a failed romance. But as Professor Colón points out, in these four novels it is his struggle to reconcile himself to the criminals' justified punishment that is most pointedly at issue. He has, by uncovering their crimes, brought about their deaths, and that is (as it should be) a genuinely weighty thing. It is a credit to Peter's character here that he recognizes the darker side of his chosen vocation.

And it is a kind of vocation that indeed is *political*. For what Peter is participating in is a core function of political authority, namely the punishment of criminals. Governments exist if for no other reason than to restrain and punish wrongdoing, and what Peter seems to recognize is just how tragic that exercise of power actually is, even when it is exercised properly. Max Weber famously invoked the idea of vocation to describe the exercise of political authority, but Weber's conception was tragic all the way through. He owed too much to Nietzsche to believe that justice was anything more than convention, and so on his account, those who hold political office do so with the deep knowledge that they cannot ultimately justify it, but that it must still be done. It is simply necessary.[3] This sense of politics as a tragic, unjustified, and necessary practice permeates our late-modern or postmodern or whatever-modern world.

I think Peter exemplifies something quite different, something more akin to what Augustine offers us in book 19 of *City of God*. In chapter six of that book, Augustine describes the dilemmas that

---

[3]See Max Weber, "Politics as Vocation," in *Essays on Sociology* (New York: Oxford University Press, 1946), 77-128.

inevitably faced judges in the ancient world, namely that the duties attendant to the ordinary exercise of their office inevitably required them to participate in terrible acts, to include torture and the execution of the innocent. Who would be a judge under these sorts of conditions? Augustine suggests that the "wise man" will, for "society drags him to his duty."[4] Augustine's dark lesson is clear: the social order, without which we cannot live or flourish, inevitably inextricably requires terrible things, things that in ordinary life we simply do not permit and that none of us should easily endorse. Peter is, I think, much in this same position, inhabiting (if only informally) political office and sending men to their deaths on account of their wrongdoing. And like Augustine's judge, he feels compelled to continue because his social order cannot endure absent the restraint of wrongdoing. But unlike, say, a Weber or Hobbes or Machiavelli, it is not *just* necessity that drives Peter, for as with the torturing judge, he is not just "wise"; he is "piously wise." He cries out in grief and loss and wants to be delivered from these necessities, to be relieved of this terrible vocation.

Where is the joy in this? The exuberance? The childlikeness? It is tempting to say that it has no place, and in some sense I think that might be correct. Peter's melancholy is well earned and wise in its own way. But inasmuch as there are always those—hucksters and utopians, remember—who promise a political order "without remainder," without tragedy, so too there are also those, perhaps dystopians and hucksters of a different sort, who see nothing but tragedy, nothing but the gloom of power clashing against power in a forever twilight struggle. They are just as mistaken, for tragedy is not the end of the

---

[4]Augustine, *Political Writings*, trans. Michael W. Tkacz and Douglas Kries (Indianapolis: Hackett, 1994).

story, not with Harriet and Peter, nor with Augustine, nor with politics more broadly.

Consider this: what finally draws Harriet out of her despondency? It is the genuine, decent, peculiar, imperfect, and (in some sense) profoundly ordinary community in Oxford. Or, to put it a bit more precisely, it is her *friends* in Oxford (and eventually, Peter). There is a kind of politics in Oxford, and it must, in the end, punish the wrongdoer; that is a tragic, if proper, necessity. But it is also proper to say that there is a kind of politics in Oxford that helps revive Harriet through her friendships and her work. It is in a political community where she can recover her dignity, self-respect, and capacity to love.

To be altogether too quick about this, to eschew the tragedy in our politics is to ignore what politics this side of the eschaton *must* do. It is to ignore the good grounds for Peter's melancholia. To suppose that tragedy is all it *can* do is to similarly ignore its possibilities and unreasonably eschew its crucial role in our flourishing. It is to try and do without hope. Augustine, after all, does not leave us with *just* the picture of the despondent judge or tragic politics but notes it merely (!) as an episode, a waypoint in God's redemption of all creation. Politics does not save, but neither does it just destroy. We would do well in our age—when our political conceptions seem to veer wildly between those two poles—to recover a sense of political possibilities and limits.

To gesture at something in closing, let me suggest a way to do some of that recovery. Friendship, I have intimated here, serves as a kind of linchpin for connecting joy and community. *Civic* friendship, the settled sense that we owe one another respect, esteem, consideration, or the like simply because we happen to belong to a common political community, might likewise serve as a kind of linchpin for navigating between tragedy and possibility. Civic friendship does not (or should not) pretend to the same sorts of goods appropriate to friendship proper; we are too disparate, too divided for that. But it might, properly understood, help us to see one another and see ourselves, as Harriet came to see herself again, as creatures lovingly made in the image of God, possessing an inviolate dignity, and fellow participants in the always imperfect, often fractious and even tragic, effort to forge a common life here together. That is not, I should say, an especially high bar, and it certainly doesn't promise the sort of exuberant joy that makes Peter such an attractive character. But it is not so bad, and these days, that is nothing to sneeze at.

CONTRIBUTORS

Christine Colón (PhD, University of California at Davis) is professor of English at Wheaton College. She is the author of *Writing for the Masses: Dorothy L. Sayers and the Victorian Literary Tradition* and *Joanna Baillie and the Art of Moral Influence* and the coauthor of *Singled Out: Why Celibacy Must Be Reinvented in Today's Church*.

Tiffany Eberle Kriner (PhD, University of Wisconsin-Madison) is associate professor of English at Wheaton College, where she teaches American literature and literature and theology. She is the author of *The Future of the Word: An Eschatology of Reading*.

Andy Mangin (MFA, Southern Methodist University) is an associate lecturer of theater at Wheaton College, where he also serves as the production manager of Arena Theater. He is also the cofounder and artistic director of Wheaton's Shakespeare in the Park.

Bryan T. McGraw (PhD, Harvard University) is associate professor of politics and international relations and dean of social sciences at Wheaton College. He is the author of *Faith in Politics: Religion and Liberal Democracy* and the coeditor of *Natural Law and Evangelical Political Thought*, and his work has appeared in *Perspectives on Political Science, Critical Review of Social and Political Philosophy,* and *Political Studies*.

AUTHOR INDEX

Akhtar, Ayad, 78-79
Alighieri, Dante, 61, 63, 85, 95-97
Auden, W. H., 8-9, 11
Augustine, 124-26
Barfield, Owen, xiv
Bernstein, Lennie, 122
Bray, Suzanne, 61, 67, 99
Brook, Peter, 78
Brown, Janice, 108
Chesterton, G. K., xii, xiv
Donne, John, 110, 115
Downing, Crystal, 50-51, 58
Edwards, Martin, 92-93
Gillis, Stacy, 13
Hannay, Margaret P., 99
Hart, Carolyn G., 99
Ingraham, Christopher, 122
James, P. D., 119
Lambourne, Norah, 83-84
Lewis, C. S., xii, xiv-xv, xvii, 85-87
Lewis, Ethan, 14, 22, 26
MacDonald, George, xiv
McGregor, Robert Kuhn, 14, 22, 26
McManis, Douglas R., 34
Mead, Marjorie Lamp, 84
Miller, Arthur, 79
Rahn's, B. J., 99
Ray, Laura K., 99
Reynolds, Barbara, xi, 61, 89, 96-97, 117
Sayers, Dorothy L., xi-xiv, 4-6, 43-44,
   67-68, 83-84, 89-91
   Begin Here, 6-7, 28
   Busman's Honeymoon, xii, 68, 110-16
   Clouds of Witness, 11, 27
   "Dogma Is the Drama, The," 45-46
   Emperor Constantine, The, 47, 51-52,
      56-60, 67
   Gaudy Night, 10, 94-95, 98-99, 104-10
   Have His Carcase, 33-39, 102-4
   Just Vengeance, The, 60-67, 69
   Man Born to Be King, The, 3
   Mind of the Maker, The, 3, 9, 27-29, 94
   Murder Must Advertise, 14-20, 27
   Nine Tailors, The, 1-2, 29-30, 82-83,
      116-17
   Strong Poison, 22-27, 98-102, 111,
      121-22
   Unpleasantness at the Bellona Club,
      The, 12-14, 17, 20, 27
   Whose Body?, 11, 13, 20-22, 27
   Why Work?, xiii, 27, 29-31
   Zeal of Thy House, The, 41-42, 47-57,
      67-68, 74-76, 82, 117
Shakespeare, William, 78, 95
Stein, Thomas Michael, 14
Taylor, D. J., 16
Tolkien, J.R.R., xii, xiv-xvi
Twenge, Jean, 123
Weber, Max, 124-25
Williams, Charles, xii, xiv, 61, 66, 85, 95-96

SUBJECT INDEX

action, xvii, 2-3, 17, 28-31, 33-40, 42-43, 57, 73-74, 81-82, 117
actors, 5, 69, 75-77, 81
arch, 41-42, 45-47, 54-55, 67, 71, 80-82
art/artistry/artists, xi-xiii, 1-3, 27, 31, 81
atonement, 60-61, 64-67, 72
audience, 32, 48, 52, 67, 73-81, 96
bodies/corpses, 33, 37-40
Bright Young People, 14-19
catharsis, 9, 80
change ringing, 1-2, 30, 82-83
Christian/Christianity, xi-xii, xiv, 3, 5, 7, 36, 43-47, 51-52, 58-72, 82-83, 95, 97, 117, 122
church, the, xii-xiii, 42, 44-45, 51-52, 56-57, 63, 65, 67, 69-71, 74, 81, 111
collaboration, 32, 68, 74, 77-79
communities/community, xii-xiv
   academic, 98, 106-10
   of action, 1-40, 42-43, 82, 117
   of faith, 41-74, 82-83, 117
   of joy, 82-127
comradeship, 89, 92
creativity/creative mind/creative power, 3, 5, 7, 28-29, 32, 34, 54, 89
creed, 61-63
Detection Club, xii, 4, 90-93
detective(s), 11-13, 20-21, 27, 29, 33, 35, 91, 94, 119
detective fiction, xii, 3, 7-10, 29, 31-33, 37, 90, 93-94, 98, 120
disintegration, 43-47
dissatisfaction, 19-20
division(s), 46-48, 50, 52
dogma/doctrine/creed, 42, 44-47, 51-52, 57-58, 83
dysfunction, 16
escapism, xvi, 10, 93-94
evil, 7-11
faith, xi-xii, 2, 41-47, 51, 56-60, 67-68, 71-72, 82-83, 117
forgiveness, 59, 67, 97
friendship, 84-85, 87-89, 123, 126-27
fun, 83, 89, 93-96, 101-3
gifts, 33-34, 36, 40, 47
God, xiii, 6-7, 28-30, 36-37, 44-45, 48, 51-66, 71, 77, 84, 88, 97, 117, 126-27
good, xi, xiii, 44, 46-48, 52-55, 57, 60, 64, 67, 74, 113-14, 117, 122-23
Holy Spirit, xii, 28, 58

hope, xv, xvii, 57, 59-61, 64, 79, 99, 116-17, 120-21, 126
humanity, 6, 39, 61, 64-65, 79-80
individual/individualism, xii-xiii, 2-3, 5-7, 10, 22, 27-31, 37, 42-43, 47, 50-53, 56-58, 61, 65-67, 69-70, 82, 96, 107, 110, 116-17, 122
Inklings, xii
innocence, 9, 11-12, 23, 62-64, 100
integrity, 3, 31, 49, 53, 95, 99, 104-6, 108-9, 114-17
jealousy, 15, 48, 100, 108
Jesus, 44-45, 56, 61, 64-65
joy, 2, 83-85, 88-89, 92, 95-99, 101-27
justice, 62-64, 124
keystone, 42, 45-47, 48, 52, 54-55, 57, 67, 71, 81-83
laugh/laughing/laughter, 52, 76, 80, 83-84, 89
letter(s), 5, 84-87, 94
Mutual Admiration Society, 4
Nicene Creed, 51, 57-58
Oxford, 89, 98, 104-6, 109-10, 113, 115-16, 122, 126
place, 13, 32-37, 100, 107-9, 112, 115, 120, 122
playwright, xi, 4, 41, 43, 47, 68-69, 75, 78-79
political, 119-20, 124-26
prayer, 53, 58, 73-74
pride, 48, 54-56
reconcile, 45, 61, 66, 124
rivalries, 15, 48
sacrifice, 59, 64-67
salvation, 56, 59-60, 96
setting, 32-37, 102
sin, 9, 46-67, 79, 95
spirit/spiritual, 15, 28-29, 53, 61, 76, 95-97, 106
theater, xii, 43, 67-81, 120
theology, 3, 32-34, 46
tragedy, 64, 121, 125-27
Trinity, The, 28, 36, 46
truth, xi, 3, 15, 28, 30, 44, 46, 53, 57-65, 69, 71, 80, 83, 95, 117-18
vision, xii-xiv, 27, 53, 63, 67, 72, 82, 104
vocation, xiii, 22, 27, 32, 53, 82, 116, 119, 124-25
war, 5-6, 12-14, 16-17, 19, 28, 30-31, 43-44, 60-62, 66, 92-94, 96-97
work, xi-xv, 2-5, 15-16, 18, 24, 27-35, 41-43, 48-49, 52-57, 60, 67-69, 71-72, 74, 82-83, 89, 93, 95, 108, 114-17, 122

The Marion E. Wade Center

Founded in 1965, the Marion E. Wade Center of Wheaton College, Illinois, houses a major research collection of writings and related materials by and about seven British authors: Owen Barfield, G. K. Chesterton, C. S. Lewis, George MacDonald, Dorothy L. Sayers, J. R. R. Tolkien, and Charles Williams. The Wade Center collects, preserves, and makes these resources available to researchers and visitors through its reading room, museum displays, educational programming, and publications. All of these endeavors are a tribute to the importance of the literary, historical, and Christian heritage of these writers. Together, these seven authors form a school of thought, as they valued and promoted the life of the mind and the imagination. Through service to those who use its resources and by making known the words of its seven authors, the Wade Center strives to continue their legacy.

The Hansen Lectureship Series

The Ken and Jean Hansen Lectureship is an annual lecture series named in honor of former Wheaton College trustee Ken Hansen and his wife, Jean, and endowed in their memory by Walter and Darlene Hansen. The series features three lectures per academic year by a Wheaton College faculty member on one or more of the Wade Center authors with responses by fellow faculty members.

Kenneth and Jean (née Hermann) Hansen are remembered for their welcoming home, deep appreciation for the imagination and the writings of the Wade authors, a commitment to serving others, and their strong Christian faith. After graduation from Wheaton College, Ken began working with Marion Wade in his residential cleaning business (later renamed ServiceMaster) in 1947. After Marion's death in 1973, Ken Hansen was instrumental in establishing the Marion E. Wade Collection at Wheaton College in honor of his friend and business colleague.

www.ingramcontent.com/pod-product-compliance
Lightning Source LLC
Chambersburg PA
CBHW032228080426
42735CB00008B/768